First published in 2012.

This edition published by Mortimer.
An Imprint of Welbeck Non-Fiction Limited, part of Welbeck
Publishing Group.
Based in London and Sydney.
www.welbeckpublishing.com

Copyright © 2012, 2017, 2022 Elvis Presley Enterprises, Inc.
Text, design and layout copyright © 2012, 2017, 2022 Welbeck
Publishing Group.

EPE, Reg. U.S. Pat & TM Off. Elvis and Elvis Presley are
registered trademarks with the U.S. Pat & TM Off.

Elvis images used by permission, Elvis Presley Enterprises, Inc.

A CIP catalogue record for this book is available from the British
Library.

ISBN 978-1-83861-099-9

10 9 8 7 6 5 4 3

Printed and bound in Dubai

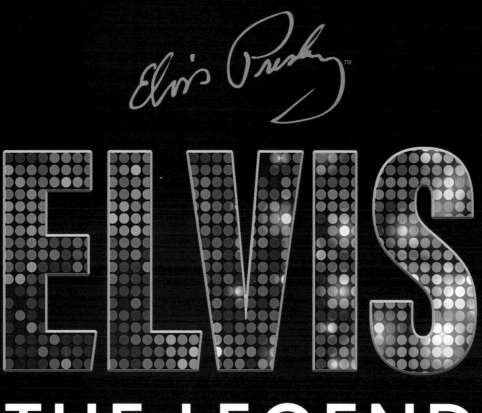

ELVIS
THE LEGEND

THE AUTHORIZED BOOK FROM THE GRACELAND® ARCHIVES

Gillian G. Gaar

MORTIMER

CONTENTS

FOREWORD

In the mid-1970s, bassist/producer Norbert Putnam was in England, producing an album by the band Splinter, who were on George Harrison's label Dark Horse. Norbert, a huge Beatles fan, never hesitated to pepper George with questions about the Fab Four whenever they were together.

One evening George finally told him, "Well, I'll make you a deal. You answer all of my questions about Elvis, and I'll answer all of your questions about the Beatles," knowing that Norbert had played bass on a number of Elvis's records. The two talked long into the night, Norbert listening with fascination as George recalled how nervous he and the other Beatles had been when they first met Elvis, at a legendary meeting in Los Angeles on August 25, 1965. In 1972, when Elvis played a historic run of shows at Madison Square Garden, George attended and was still nervous when he went to see Elvis after the show. "I went backstage, and I'm waiting in line, and Elvis comes up, and I couldn't talk!" he told Norbert. "Did all of the Beatles feel that way about Elvis?" Norbert asked. "Oh yeah," George replied. "Elvis was it. Everyone else was secondary."

It was the kind of response Elvis had generated from the moment he first burst into the public eye. When DJ Dewey Phillips played an acetate of Elvis' first record, "That's All Right" on Memphis radio station WHBQ on July 8, 1954 — a mere three days after the song had been recorded — there was an instantaneous reaction from the listeners who knew: Elvis was it. Phone calls began coming into the station asking for the record to be played again. And again. And again. Everyone else was secondary.

And that's pretty much the way it went for the rest of Elvis' career. As the first star of rock 'n' roll, he made everyone else secondary. He set a standard that is still being emulated today. In music, as artists continue to rework rock 'n' roll, the genre that Elvis helped pioneer. In style, where the pegged trousers Elvis wore in the 1950s, the leather suit seen in his 1960s TV special Elvis, and the jumpsuits of the 1970s aren't seen as "retro" outfits, but something classic, iconic. In the very

idea of what it means to be a rock star: living large, with his own custom-made jewelry and sunglasses; a lavish Southern mansion; planes, trains, and automobiles at his disposal; and always surrounded by a loyal entourage of family and friends. As the ads for the 2002 album *ELV1S: 30 #1 Hits* put it, "Before anyone did anything, Elvis did everything."

As a rock fan, there's never been a time I didn't know who Elvis Presley was. But I didn't really start to get Elvis until 1973, when "Hound Dog" came blasting out of the TV set during a commercial; riveted by the exciting sound, I went out and bought the single the next day. There have been many more record (and video, and CD, and DVD) purchases since. And then there's been the fun of discovering who Elvis was (with Peter Guralnick's masterful two-volume biography, *Last Train To Memphis* and *Careless Love* being must-reads for every Elvis fan), debating the merits of one record or film over another, visiting Graceland, and attending Elvis Week. Most exciting has been the opportunity to talk with people who knew and worked with Elvis, including his original musicians, Scotty Moore and D.J. Fontana; Steve Binder, the director of the 1968 *Elvis* TV special; and musicians Jerry Scheff and Ronnie Tutt, who performed with Elvis in the 1970s, to mention only a few.

But of course it's Elvis' work that continues to provide the greatest thrill. And the pleasure in writing this book comes from being able to write about some of the greatest music, films, and performances in rock history, and the man who brought it all together.

We hope you enjoy this look at one of the most remarkable personalities of the twentieth century, a man whose accomplishments continue to dazzle people today, whether they're longtime fans or people just discovering the work of a legend: Elvis Presley.

— Gillian G. Gaar, Seattle, WA

INTRODUCTION

There aren't many people that are known around the world by just their first name. But such is the case with Elvis. You don't need to say "Elvis Presley"; just say "Elvis" and everyone knows exactly who you're talking about.

It's not quite as easy to say who Elvis was, because he meant different things to different people. Some people knew him as a member of their family: a son, a husband, a father. Other people knew him as a friend, a school pal, a boyfriend. To some he was a fellow musician; to others he was a fellow soldier. To those who benefitted from his generosity, he was a much needed helping hand.

The many people that crossed his path continue to treasure their memories of Elvis. Some recall the shy, sandy haired kid who brought his guitar to school, and who, if you asked enough, might play a song for you. Others remember the teenager who frequented the Memphis record shops, flipping through the new releases, smiling every time the little demonstration record he'd given to the owner for the store's jukebox came on, never boasting to the other shoppers that it was his voice they were listening to. Neighbors recall a young man who was always respectful to his parents, and eager to do what he could to make their lives a little easier. Friends remember Elvis as someone who was as enthusiastic about touch football as he was about attending all-night gospel singings.

Elvis' first serious girlfriend, Dixie Locke, remembers how Elvis just couldn't get enough of music. On Sundays, it wasn't enough to enjoy the music at their own church; they'd sneak out and visit the African-American churches to listen to their music too. Or they would spend hours in the listening booths at the record store playing records, with Dixie trying to help Elvis remember the lyrics to new songs. A love of music was key to many of Elvis' relationships. His friend Charlie Hodge, who met Elvis in the army, helped to cheer him up in the months after his mother's death. But they really bonded over their mutual interest in music — Charlie being a performer too — and the two would play and sing together throughout the years of their friendship, with Charlie joining Elvis' stage band in the 1970s. Both Steve Binder, who directed Elvis

in the 1968 television special Elvis, and Chips Moman, who produced Elvis in early 1969 at American Sound Studios in Memphis, were quick to pick up on Elvis' deep love of music, and his equally strong desire to create great music of his own, which made them just as determined to help Elvis make some of the best work of his career with them. Musicians who worked with Elvis in the studio recall his perseverance as he pushed himself through take after take. At one session, after 26 takes of 'Hound Dog', producer Steve Sholes was satisfied, but Elvis wasn't. He wanted to keep going, and did, for another five takes, before finally announcing "This is the one." Elvis knew what he wanted and kept on working until he got it. His reward in this case was another Number One record.

There was also a playful side to Elvis. He had always shared what he could with his friends, and once he began to make a bit of money he couldn't wait to share his good fortune with those around him. Friends recall the many parties he hosted, and how during his seasons in Las Vegas he'd bring everybody up to his suite for sing-alongs that lasted until dawn. There were trips to Hawaii where he picked up the tab for everyone. And who could forget being given a car by Elvis? Friends, employees, even total strangers received cars when Elvis was feeling generous. Longtime friend Jerry Schilling was even given a house by the man he'd long looked up to and admired, recalling Elvis' simple reasoning for the gift: "You never had a home. I wanted to be the one to give it to you."

But "shy" was the most common word people used to describe Elvis in the early days; to his first producer, Sam Phillips, "He was beyond shy." Yet Sam sensed something else beneath the surface, something he couldn't put his finger on, but wanted to tap into. His patience was rewarded after hours of rehearsal when Elvis suddenly felt a newfound freedom, and unexpectedly broke into 'That's All Right.' Guitarist Scotty Moore and bassist Bill Black fell in right behind him, and rock 'n' roll would never be the same again.

RIGHT: Elvis in his dressing room while working on the film *Harum Scarum*, 1965.

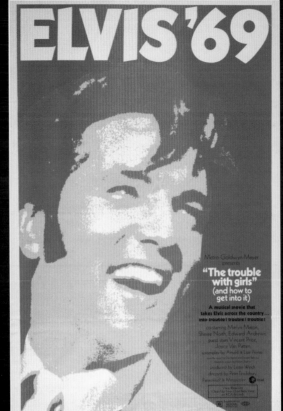

And this is the moment when most people's memories of Elvis begin. For most people knew Elvis as a performer. His music first won over people in Memphis, then in the South, then across the country, then around the world. He was the newly-crowned King of Rock 'n' roll, and people still remember the first time they heard a classic song like 'Heartbreak Hotel', or 'Don't Be Cruel', or 'Jailhouse Rock'. For some, that first moment might have been seeing one of Elvis' TV appearances, or one of his movies. A very fortunate number of people were lucky enough to actually see him perform live, dazzling audiences in a way that just can't be experienced on record or the small (or big) screen.

Other fans had their first memory of Elvis come a little later. Perhaps it was when they saw the 1968 television special, a show that reaffirmed Elvis' status as one of rock 'n' roll's best performers. Or maybe it came during the 1970s, at a show in Las Vegas or another sold out concert. And he was a bigger global phenomenon too. There was a reason Elvis was tapped for the first global satellite broadcast of a rock show, the *Aloha From Hawaii* concert held in January 1973; everyone knew that with Elvis on board, the show would receive top ratings.

Elvis' greatest impact was as a performer. He helped elevate rock 'n' roll from what was virtually an underground style into a music that reverberated around the entire world. He helped to develop an entirely new genre of music, and so changed the course of popular music forever. Elvis' music, his visual image, his fashion style influenced countless performers who have come after him — sometimes simply seeing Elvis play guitar was enough to inspire people to pick up instrument themselves. Even Elvis' catchphrases have passed into public consciousness. After all, what do you think of when you hear the words "Thank you. Thank you very much"? Chances are, it's Elvis.

For all these, and countless other reasons, Elvis will always be remembered. Those who were closest to him, his family and his friends, will always feel the strongest connection, and have the most personal memories. But anyone who was ever touched by Elvis, whether through his music, or his live performances, or his many acts of kindness, feels that they know him a little bit too. How could it be otherwise? Elvis had always been there for them, from the beginning, never hesitating to stop and pose for a photo, sign an autograph, have a chat, wave hello. Small gestures, perhaps. But Elvis was always there for his fans. And Elvis' fans will always be there for him.

ABOVE LEFT: Advertisement for Elvis' show at Sicks Stadium, Seattle (September 1, 1957). A young Jimi Hendrix attended the performance.

ABOVE RIGHT: A very "mod" look for this film poster for one of Elvis' last films, *The Trouble With Girls (And How To Get Into It).*

RIGHT: Elvis greets his fans on the set of *Love Me Tender.*

FROM THE DEEP COUNTRY TO THE BIG CITY

Elvis Aaron Presley was born in a small, two-room shotgun shack in East Tupelo, Mississippi, on January 8, 1935. (East Tupelo would later be incorporated with its neighboring town, Tupelo, in 1946.) His parents were Gladys and Vernon Presley. If you'd told the small family that one day their son would buy them a home whose living room would be larger than the entire East Tupelo house they lived in it would have seemed unlikely. Life was hard for the Presleys. Elvis' twin, christened Jessie Garon Presley, had died at birth. He was buried in an unmarked grave in the local cemetery, as there was no money for a proper burial. There was never enough money to go around.

But the bond the family shared was something that money couldn't buy, and Elvis had all the love and support he needed as he grew up. His interest in music was clear from an early age — his mother recalled him running down the aisle to try and sing with the church choir when he was two — and his parents never failed to offer him encouragement. His first public performance came about when a teacher at his school, Mrs. Oleta Grimes, heard him singing at school. Mrs. Grimes took him to the principal, who entered him in a talent contest held on Children's Day at the Mississippi-Alabama Fair and Dairy Show held at the Tupelo Fairgrounds. On October 3, 1945, Elvis faced his first audience, standing on a chair to reach the microphone, and, singing acapella because he had no guitar, sang Red Foley's 'Old Shep,' a tearjerker about a boy and his beloved dog. The simple, unadorned performance undoubtedly tugged on the heartstrings. Elvis took fifth place in the competition, winning $5 in ride tickets, but his main memory of the event was being punished by his mother for going on one of the wilder rides without permission.

A few months later Elvis received a guitar for his 11th birthday. His uncles and his pastor at the First Assembly of God church, Frank Smith, helped him learn to play, and he was later encouraged to sing at services, though as Smith recalled, "I would have to insist … he didn't push himself." By junior high, Elvis was bringing his guitar to school, where his friends remember him playing country and gospel songs at lunchtime. "He was crazy about music," said one of his friends, James Ausborn. "That's all he talked about."

Elvis was excited to learn that James' brother was a real musician — Carvel Lee Ausborn, who performed professionally as Mississippi Slim. Slim hosted the *WELO Jamboree*, a weekly radio show broadcast from the Tupelo courthouse, and the two boys were frequent visitors. Audience members were asked to perform on the show as well, and Elvis did so on occasion, hanging around afterwards in the hopes of getting tips on guitar playing from Slim. The one thing everyone from Tupelo remembers about Elvis was his keen interest in music.

On November 6, 1948, the Presleys moved to Memphis in the hopes of finding better job opportunities. The atmosphere in Memphis was worlds away from that of Tupelo. Tupelo was a small town; Memphis was a city. It was so big to Elvis that when his father took him to school the first day, Elvis turned around and ran straight home, explaining that he was intimidated by all the people. Vernon told him he could stay home for one day, but had to go back to school the next. And he did.

Vernon and Gladys soon found work, and the following year the family moved into public housing

RIGHT: An early picture of Elvis, age two, with his mother and father. The photo was later used on the cover of *Elvis Country*.

at Lauderdale Courts, the biggest, and nicest, place they'd ever lived in. It was not too far from Humes High School, where Elvis was finally settling in, volunteering in the library, joining the ROTC in 10th grade, and briefly playing football for the Humes High Tigers.

He also palled around with a gang of friends who lived in the neighborhood. The mother of one friend, Jesse Lee Denson, persuaded her son to help Elvis with his guitar playing. Lee's friends were also aspiring musicians; there were the Burnette brothers, Johnny and Dorsey, as well as Johnny Black, whose older brother, Bill, played in a country group called the Starlite Wranglers. When he wasn't riding his bike or playing touch football, Elvis would play guitar with the other boys, sitting in the background, but joining

LEFT: A studious looking Elvis at 11 years of age.

RIGHT: A teenage Elvis posing with a toy gun outside of the Lauderdale Courts apartment complex in Memphis. He would later collect many real firearms.

Elvis Presley

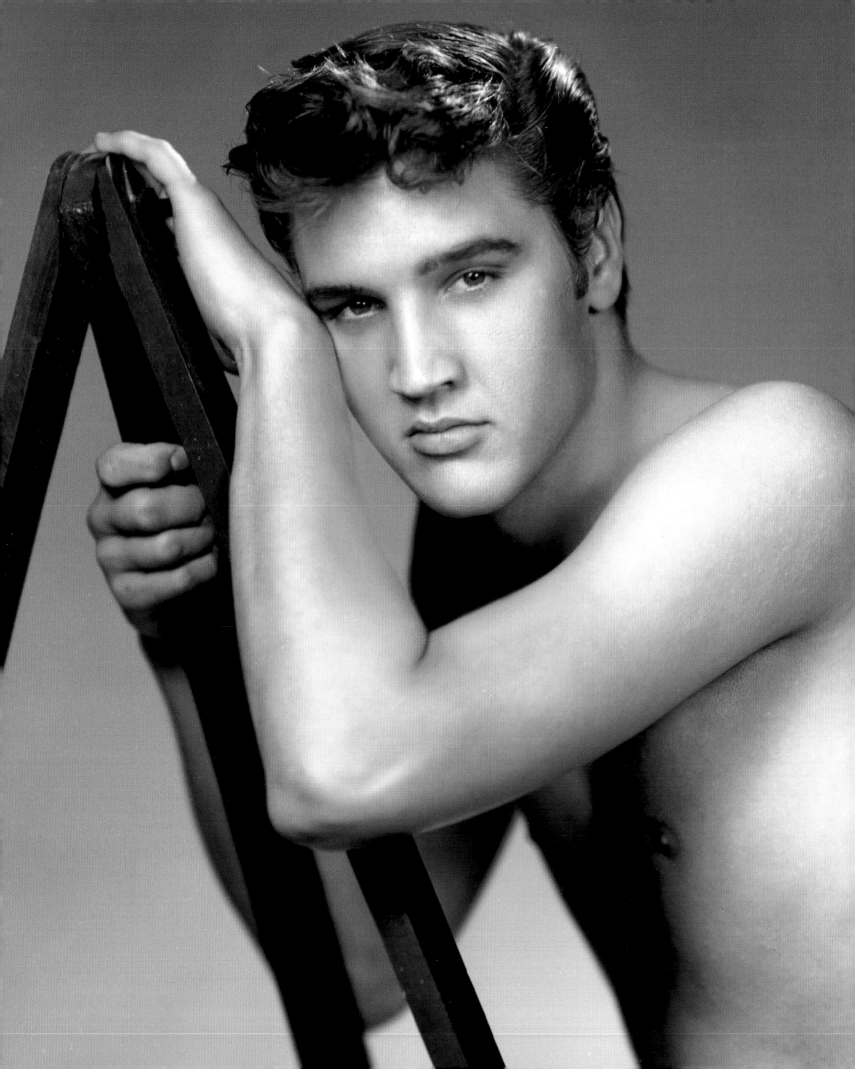

in nonetheless. He'd also play at parties, though he was sometimes too shy to perform when all the lights were on. So it came as a surprise to one of his friends when, during an organized visit to the local hospital, Elvis brought his guitar to sing to the patients.

It was equally a surprise to his schoolmates when Elvis performed at Humes High's Annual Minstrel Show during his senior year, on April 9, 1953. Most students didn't even know he played guitar. And having his name misspelled in the program as "Elvis Prestly" couldn't have helped his nerves. Elvis performed 'Till I Waltz Again With You,' a song made popular by Teresa Brewer, and so impressed the audience he was called back for an encore. Ballads, country, and gospel songs were still the kind of songs he preferred to perform. One of his teachers later recalled Elvis playing guitar quietly at a school picnic, but although playing for himself, he gradually attracting the attention of the other students: "There was something about his quiet, plaintive singing which drew them like a magnet." Elvis wasn't yet in the spotlight, but he had already learned how to make an impression with his music.

Elvis graduated from high school on June 3, 1953, and by early July he'd landed a job at M.B. Parker Machinists. But he was still thinking about music. That same month, an article appeared in the *Memphis Press-Scimitar* about a group of inmates, The Prisonaires, who'd been escorted to Memphis for the day to cut a record at the Memphis Recording Service (later to be renamed Sun Studio). Was this where Elvis learned about the studio and its owner, producer Sam Phillips? Sam, originally from Alabama, had opened the Memphis Recording Service in 1950 specifically to work with African-American performers. He was soon working with an impressive roster of talent, including Howlin' Wolf, B.B. King, and Rufus Thomas, and in 1952 he'd started his own label, Sun Records.

OPPOSITE: A teen idol in the making, early 1950s.

BELOW: A receipt from Elvis for a payment by his manager "Colonel" Tom Parker; the notation indicates how the payment was broken down for Elvis and his band, Scotty Moore, Bill Black, and DJ Fontana.

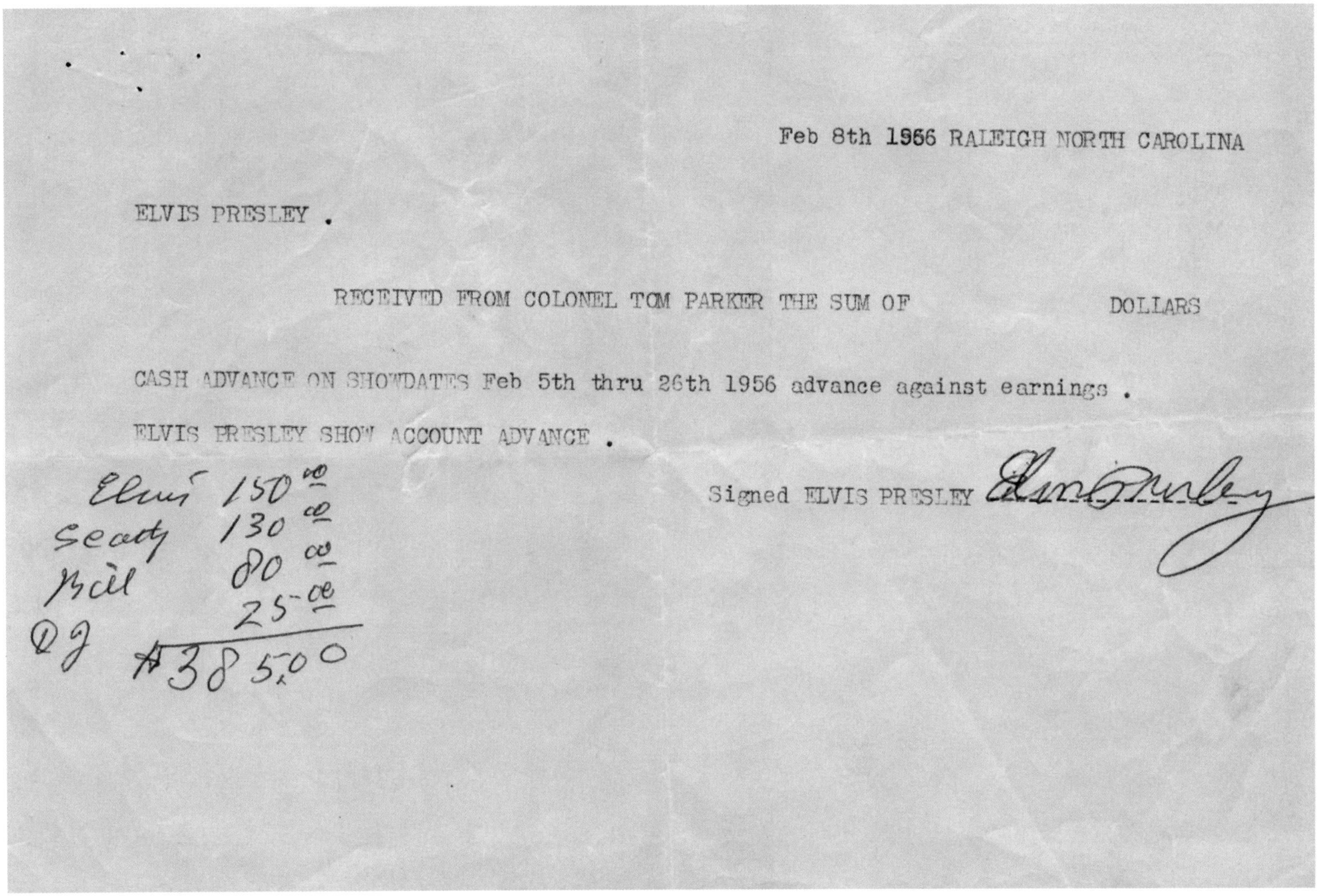

Feb 8th 1956 RALEIGH NORTH CAROLINA

ELVIS PRESLEY .

RECEIVED FROM COLONEL TOM PARKER THE SUM OF   DOLLARS

CASH ADVANCE ON SHOWDATES Feb 5th thru 26th 1956 advance against earnings .

ELVIS PRESLEY SHOW ACCOUNT ADVANCE .

Signed ELVIS PRESLEY

Elvis 150.00
Scotty 130.00
Bill 80.00
DJ 25.00
$385.00

Business cards for the studio boasted, "We record anything — anywhere — anytime." One of those services was making personal recordings; for $8.25, anyone could come in the studio and record a two-sided acetate. Elvis had never spoken to anyone about making a career in music, but it's not insignificant that he was drawn to a business run by a man who known for doing something different. Elvis saved his money and decided to make a record at the studio; "I just wanted to hear what I sounded like," he explained.

It was a big step for the naturally reserved young man to take. "I took the guitar, and I watched people, and I learned to play a little bit," he later said. "But I would never sing in public. I was very shy about it, you know." Now he was ready to find out what he could do.

The Music That Made The Man

Elvis was heralded as the King of Rock 'n' roll — rock 'n' roll being a music that drew on country swing and gritty rhythm & blues. But there was a lot more to his musical makeup than just those two genres.

The very first music Elvis heard were the gospel hymns at his local church, the First Assembly of God, and gospel would be his favorite music for the rest of his life. When the family moved to Memphis, Elvis became a regular at the All-Night Gospel Singings held at the Ellis Auditorium, seeing acts like the Speer Family and the Sunshine Boys. The Blackwood Brothers were local heroes, whom Elvis not only saw at the Gospel Singings and heard on the WMPS radio show *High Noon Round-Up*, but also knew as members of the Assembly of God church he attended in Memphis. He was especially fond of the Statesmen, whose lively performances electrified audiences. It wasn't just their vocal acrobatics that impressed Elvis; he also took note of the furor that resulted when bass singer Jim "Big Chief" Wetherington would jiggle his legs during a performance.

Country music was another important element in Elvis' musical education. In Tupelo he was in the audience for the *WELO Jamboree* radio show as often as he could be, waiting for his chance to talk to the

show's host, Mississippi Slim. Along with gospel, Elvis' friends remember him singing country songs when he performed at school breaks and parties. Eddy Arnold was a big favorite, as were Hank Williams, Roy Acuff and Ernest Tubb.

Rhythm & blues had its roots in gospel, and also laid the groundwork for soul, all styles that Elvis could appreciate. In Memphis, the musically curious could turn their radio dials to WDIA, "The Mother Station of the Negroes," the first radio station in the country with an all-black air staff. Elvis could listen to future R&B stars B.B. King or Rufus Thomas spin records by Howlin' Wolf or Fats Domino. Over at WHBQ, Dewey Phillips — "Daddy-O-Dewey" — dazzled Memphis listeners with his non-stop patter and diverse musical taste on his *Red, Hot And Blue* radio show, which leaned heavily (but not exclusively) on R&B. Perhaps Elvis first heard the voices of two singers he admired, Clyde McPhatter or Roy Hamilton on Dewey's show.

Pop artists, far easier to find on the radio, also captured Elvis' attention. He was a big fan of Dean Martin, and friends remember him singing songs by Bing Crosby, Kay Starr and Teresa Brewer. He also had a fondness for Eddie Fisher and Perry Como.

Nor did he ignore classical music. The big dramatic ballads he was partial to in his '70s concerts certainly showed the influence of singers like Roy Hamilton, but also the operatic stylings of Mario Lanza and Enrico Caruso as well. And he frequently went to the Overton Park Shell, an outdoor venue in Memphis, to hear the orchestra, fascinated by how long the musicians could play, the conductor so confident he didn't need to look at the score. He listened to the Metropolitan Opera, and there were classical albums in his record collection as well.

"I just loved music," Elvis said of his musical tastes. He fully appreciated a good song or good singer whatever the genre, as long as the passion was there; what he couldn't stand were singers that were "all technique and no emotional feeling." Elvis' openness to the diverse influences around him gave him a palette to draw upon when he began creating his own music.

RIGHT: Elvis behind the piano in the studio during *King Creole* sessions. He occasionally played piano on his recordings.

RISING SUN

The songs Elvis recorded for Sun Records laid the foundation for the rest of his career.
They also contain some of his most original and innovative work.

The first two records were the acetates he recorded for his own private use, and the four songs — 'My Happiness,' 'That's When Your Heartaches Begin,' 'I'll Never Stand In Your Way,' and 'It Wouldn't Be The Same Without You' — were gentle numbers, the kind of sweet songs it's easy to imagine Elvis singing to his teenage girlfriends. And the plaintive, yearning quality in his vocal is very much present in 'Harbor Lights,' recorded at his first professional session with Scotty Moore and Bill Black on July 5, 1954.

But it's with 'That's All Right,' recorded at that same session, where his legend really begins. It's here that Elvis finally kicks off his restraints and fully gives himself to the music, sounding positively giddy by the last verse. The song was paired with 'Blue Moon of Kentucky' on the single, two tracks that complemented each other perfectly: Arthur "Big Boy" Crudup's blues number goosed up by a country beat, and Bill Monroe's country tune jazzed up with the blues. It was a mixing and melding of different musical styles in the same song that typified Elvis' work at Sun.

The next Sun single, 'Good Rockin' Tonight'/'I Don't Care If The Sun Don't Shine,' takes the same approach in blending musical genres, and exudes even more confidence. Elvis ushers in Roy Brown's R&B number 'Good Rockin' Tonight' with an extended "W-e-l-l-l," before sliding into a jaunty romp, boasting of his prowess as a "mighty mighty man." He has even more fun on the teasing flip side, which came from a most unusual source — Dean Martin sings it in the film *Scared Stiff.*

There's an underlying playfulness in all of Elvis' Sun records, something made explicit on his next single, 'Milkcow Blues Boogie.' The song starts off in a slow, meandering fashion, when Elvis brings it to a halt, stating, "Hold it, fellas. That don't *move.* Let's get real, real *gone* for a change!" Another extended

"W-e-l-l-l…" and the song takes off at a rollicking gallop. Similarly, the flipside, 'You're A Heartbreaker,' is ostensibly a song about a breakup, but Elvis sounds far too jocular to be downhearted about the matter.

And he's undeniably frisky as he asks his former love to return on the next single, 'Baby Let's Play House,' teasing for all he's worth, and making it sound like its his girlfriend's loss if she doesn't change her mind. The B-side, 'I'm Left, You're Right, She's Gone' holds the distinction of being the first Elvis song to feature drums, and it was the first original number Elvis recorded as well, written by Stan Kesler at Sam Phillips' request. The musicians first tried it as a slower blues, but ultimately went for an upbeat country arrangement.

Kesley also co-wrote Elvis' last Sun single, 'I Forgot To Remember To Forget,' another country-influenced song with some clever word play. And the B-side, Junior Parker's 'Mystery Train,' has a driving beat emulating the locomotive of the song coupled with one of Elvis' most carefree vocals — just listen to him letting out an exuberant "Woo!" at the end.

The last song Elvis recorded at Sun was the bluesy 'When It Rains, It Really Pours,' a session cut short when the sale of his contract to RCA was announced. Elvis' time at Sun was over. The tracks he recorded during that historic two year period would be released in various configurations over the years, including the comprehensive collection *Sunrise* (1999). For anyone with an interest in Elvis, the Sun recordings are essential.

From Memphis To The World

When Elvis first walked through the door of the Memphis Recording Service, the first person he encountered was Marion Keisker, Sam Phillips' assistant. Marion had been a popular radio host in Memphis and Elvis was likely to have heard her before. Now he nervously made small talk with her

RIGHT: As his success grew, Elvis had to get used to signing autographs.

SUN. FEB. 5th MOSQUE 2 SHOWS 2:30-8:30

Laurel and Main, Richmond, Va.

RAILEY'S APPLIANCE CENTERS

Presents

ELVIS PRESLEY
IN PERSON!
and his "BLUE MOONERS"

with Guests From The
"GRAND OLE OPRY"
★★★ THE LOUVIN BROTHERS ★★★

THE CARTER SISTERS
with MOTHER MAYBELLE ★★

ROD BRASFIELD ★ JUSTIN TUBB ★ BENNY MARTIN

Tickets: Orch. $2.00 ★ Mezz. & Loge $1.50 ★ Gen. Adm. $1.00
Tickets available at Railey's Appliance Center, 1418 Hull St. and the new location at 1817 West Broad St., also at Thalhimers and Powers News Store in Petersburg, Va.

PIZZINI POSTER & PRINTING CO., RICHMOND, VA.

LEFT: Poster for a very early Elvis concert at the Mosque Theater on February 5, 1956.

RIGHT: A somber portrait from a 1950s photo session.

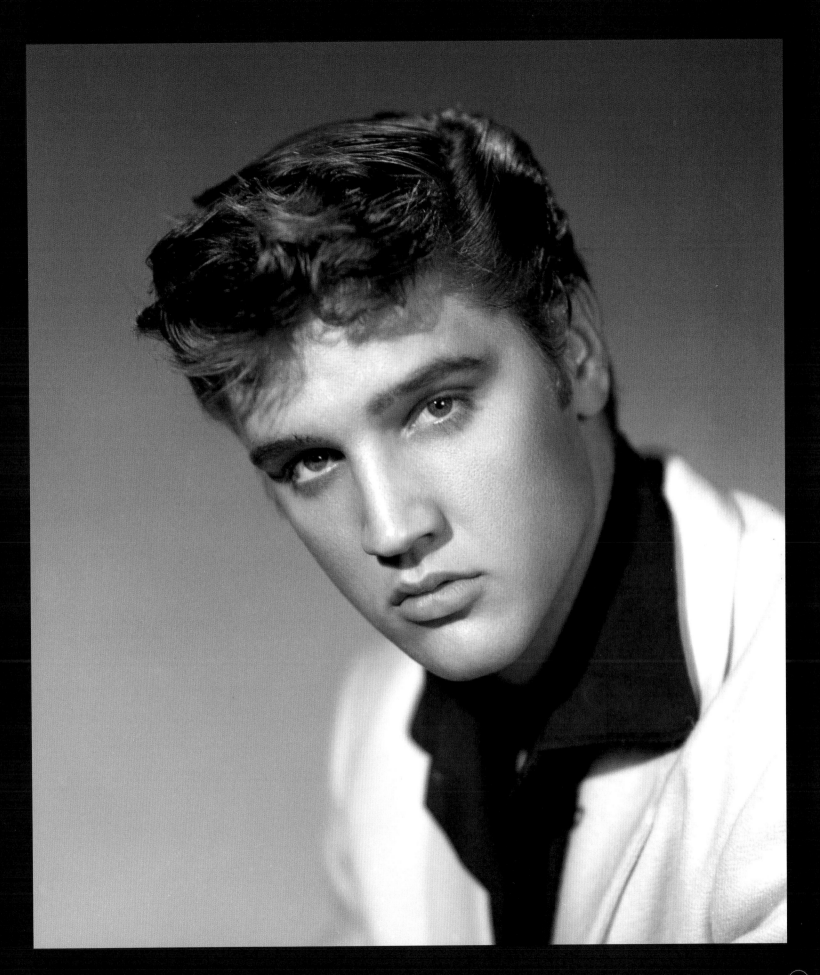

LEFT: Memphis DJ Dewey Phillips helped break Elvis on Memphis radio.

BELOW LEFT: A Paris hotel expense slip from 1959.

BELOW: Elvis had many friends in the police, and was even a deputy himself.

HOTEL PRINCE DE GALLES

NOTE DÉBOURS CONCIERGE
PORTER'S BILL .

M R. PRESLEY   N° 320

3/7	Pharmacie	.180
	Coiffeur	3.200
	Portier	10.000
	Réparation Montre	1.500
4/7	Voiture ORLY DU 3/7	9.850
4/7	Voiture Soirée du 3/7	28.000
	Portier	3.000
	Voiture	42.100
	6 Billets frankfurt	48.920
		146.150
	Ret. Billets Frankfurt	47.420
		98.730
	Voiture Frankfurt	

THE 15 % SERVICE IS NOT APPLIED ON THE PORTER'S BILL.
LE 15 % N'EST PAS APPLIQUÉ SUR LA NOTE DE DÉBOURS
DU CONCIERGE.

Elvis Presley

"ELVIS PRESLEY SHOW" IN PERSON
R C A'S TOP RECORDING STAR
WITH STARS OF THE GRAND OLE OPRY

Friedman's JEWELERS

ABOVE: Crowds gather before another sold out show.

as he waited to make his record. It was a conversation Marion would relate many times over the coming years, recalling how when Elvis asked if she knew anyone looking for a singer, she'd asked him "What kind of a singer are you?" "I sing all kinds," he told her. Trying to pin him down, Marion persisted: "Who do you sound like?" But Elvis only gave another open-ended answer: "I don't sound like nobody."

The first song he sang that day was 'My Happiness,' a pretty ballad that had been popularized by Jon and Sandra Steele in 1948, and a song that more than one of Elvis' girlfriends recalled him singing on their dates. 'My Happiness' and the other song Elvis recorded that day, the Ink Spots ballad, 'That's When Your Heartaches Begin,' each have a beguiling, almost ethereal presence. There was something about Elvis' performances that made an impression on Marion. Before he left, she made sure to write down his name (though misspelling it as Elvis "Pressley"), and made the additional notation, "Good ballad singer. Hold."

Elvis returned to the Memphis Recording Service

in January 1954 to record another acetate, the equally tender 'I'll Never Stand In Your Way' (a Top 30 hit for Joni James in 1953) and Jimmy Wakely's 'It Wouldn't Be The Same Without You.' Then he waited for something to happen. He took the records to the local record shops he frequented and was secretly thrilled when they were played on the store's jukebox. He auditioned for a local gospel quartet, the Songfellows (co-founded by Cecil Blackwood, the nephew of James Blackwood of the Blackwood Brothers Quartet), but failed to make the cut; "They said I couldn't sing," he later unhappily recalled. He made a few local appearances with his friend Ronald Smith, who also helped Elvis get a short solo spot at the Hi-Hat club. But he spent most of his time working as a delivery truck driver for the Crown Electric company and hanging out with his steady girlfriend, Dixie Locke.

Just as he began wondering if anything was ever going to break for him, he got his chance. Marion had been pestering Sam Phillips about bringing in

ballad, 'Without You,' that he thought might make a good single and on June 26, he had Marion give the young singer a call. Elvis rushed right over, but after going through what Elvis recalled as "Everything I Knew," Sam felt he wasn't quite right for 'Without You.' Instead, he contacted Scotty Moore, a guitarist in the Starlite Wranglers, and suggested he work with Elvis. So on July 4, Elvis came over the Scotty's house, where they were joined by bassist Bill Black, another member of the Starlite Wranglers, and played together for a few hours.

The trio was back at the Memphis Recording Service the following evening, little suspecting that history was about to be made. After going through the usual roster of ballads, Elvis began cutting up on a song called 'That's All Right' during a break. Bill joined in, Scotty did too, and Sam Phillips knew immediately that he'd found something fresh, new, and above all, different. The original version of 'That's All Right' was a blues number with a touch of swing, but Elvis made it jump like a live wire. A few days later the trio took the opposite approach, turning Bill Monroe's laid-back 'Blue Moon of Kentucky' into something much bolder.

The two songs became Elvis' first record, released a few weeks later in July. It created an instant sensation in Memphis. Elvis was on his way. His first big performance came at the end of the month when "Ellis" Presley (as he appeared on the posters), opened for Slim Whitman at the Overton Park Shell in Memphis. Elvis' nerves caused his legs to start shaking, which drew a big response from the crowd, leading Elvis to work more carefully on what would become his signature performing style.

The filing time shown in the date line on telegrams and day letters is STANDARD TIME at point of origin. Time of receipt is STANDARD TIME at point of destination

NL OCT 20 1955

(COPY.)

MR & MRS VERNON PRESLEY

2124 LAMAR ST PHONE 484921 MEMPHIS TENN

DEAR MR & MRS PRESLEY FOLLOWING IS THE COPY FOR THE WIRE AUTHORIZING

COL PARKER TO NEGOTIATE A RECORD CONTRACT ON BEHALF OF ELVIS.

"DEAR COL PARKER. WE HERBY AUTHORIZE YOU TO ACT AS OUR SOLE AND

EXCLUSIVE REPRESENTATIVE IN ALL NEGOTIATIONS PERTAINING TO THE RECORDING

CONTRACT OF ELVIS PRESLEY THIS AUTHORIZATION TO INCLUDE THE SETTLEMENT

FOR THE PRESENT CONTRACT WITH SUN RECORDS AND FULL AUTHORITY TO

NEGOTIATE A NEW RECORDING CONTRACT WITH A MOAJOR RECORDING FIRM

NO OTHER PERSON OR PERSONS ARE AUTHORIZED TO REPRESENT ELVIS PRESLEY

IN ANY RECORDING CONTRACT NEGOTIATIONS OTHER THAN COL PARKER AND WE

WILL BE BOUND BY YOUR DECISSION AS WE FEEL THAT YOU WILL BE FOR THE

BEST INTEREST OF ELVIS PRESLEY SIGNED MR & MRS VERNON PRESLEY AS

GUARDIANS FOR ELVIS PRESEEY". SEND THIS WIRE TO COL PARKER CARE

THE HOLIDAY MOTEL ROUTE 3 MECHANICSBURG PA, COLONEL IS NOT ONLY

INTERESTED IN GETTING ELVIS ON MAJOR LABEL BUT WANTS TO GET THE BEST,

POSSIBLE DEAL FOR HIM NOW AND FOR THE FUTURE YOU CAN BE ASSURED

THAT YOU ARE PUTTING THIS IN MOST CONFIDENT HANDS KINDEST REGARDS

TO YOU AND ELVIS

TOM DISKIS

28) Elvis Presley

Elvis' career quickly began to pick up steam. On October 2 he appeared on The Grand Ole Opry show in Nashville, and a few weeks later landed a regular Saturday night spot on the *Louisiana Hayride* radio show, performed before a live audience in Shreveport, Louisiana. For the next year, he was constantly on the road, traveling further and further afield. He first played extensively in the south: Tennessee, Louisiana, Arkansas, Texas, Mississippi, Alabama. There were a few dates up north to spread the word, and at a February 26, 1955 date in Cleveland, Elvis met influential disc jockey Bill Randle, who helped Elvis secure an audition for the TV show *Arthur Godfrey's Talent Scouts* in March.

The audition proved unsuccessful, but by this time someone else had his eye on Elvis. "Colonel" Tom Parker (an honorary title given to him by Louisiana governor Jimmie Davis), had previously managed country artist Eddy Arnold, and was looking after another country performer, Hank Snow, when he first saw Elvis. Parker arranged for Elvis to open for Hank Snow on a few tours in 1955. He observed that while Hank might be the headliner, Elvis was coming up fast.

And if anyone had any doubts about Elvis' potential, his appearance in Jacksonville, Florida, on May 13, 1955, removed them for good. At the end of his set, Elvis had teasingly announced 'Girls, I'll see you all backstage," then found himself being chased across the field by a pack of screaming teenage girls, who followed him into the locker room and tore off his jacket, shirt, and shoes. Elvis was forced to take refuge on the top of a shower stall until the police could clear the room. Parker "got dollar marks in his eyes," as his friend Mae Boren Axton recalled.

Elvis' records were beginning to have a national impact too. 'Baby Let's Play House' hit the country charts, and 'I Forgot To Remember To Forget' would actually top the country charts. It seemed only a matter of time before Elvis would move up to a major label, and Parker was helping him to field all the offers.

When Elvis arrived for the annual Country Music Disc Jockey Convention in Nashville on November 10, he found himself proclaimed Most Promising Country & Western artist by both *Billboard* and *Cash Box*. He met up again with Mae

Axton, who'd co-written a song she thought would be perfect for Elvis: 'Heartbreak Hotel.' After hearing it, Elvis was quick to agree. "Hot dog, Mae, play it again!" he said, assuring her "That's gonna be my next record."

And just 11 days later, it was finally decided who Elvis was going to make that record for: RCA, who paid $35,000 for Elvis' contract, then the largest fee ever paid for a recording artist. With a new contract, a new label, and a new song, Elvis was more than ready to face the new year.

Presleymania!

The two years from 1956 to 1957 were the most hectic time in Elvis' career. In 1956 in particular, he worked non-stop; there were live shows, TV spots, recording sessions and film work. By the end of 1957, he'd appeared on all the top-rated TV variety shows of the period, made three hit films, and became the best selling artist in RCA's history, racking up six #1 singles, three #1 EPs, and four #1 albums.

The wild ride began on January 10, 1956, two days after Elvis' 21st birthday, when he arrived at RCA's studios in Nashville for his first recording session with the label. It also the first time Elvis, Scotty, and Bill recorded with their drummer, DJ Fontana, who had played in the house band for the *Louisiana Hayride*, and had joined Elvis' band the previous August. The group, working with additional guitarist Chet Atkins, pianist Floyd Cramer, and three backing vocalists, cut five songs in two days, including the song Elvis had promised Mae Axton would be his first single: 'Heartbreak Hotel,' which was released at the end of the month.

At the same time, he made his national television debut on *Stage Show* on January 28, then spent three more days in RCA's studios in New York City recording songs for his first album. It suddenly seemed like everything was happening all at once. 'Heartbreak Hotel' took off, topping the charts and becoming Elvis' first million seller. The *Elvis Presley* album also topped the charts and quickly reached over a quarter of a million in sales. The *Stage Show* appearances were extended from four Saturdays to six. By the end of March, Elvis had shot a screen test and was negotiating to make his first motion picture.

OPPOSITE: Telegram from Tom Diskis to Elvis' mother and father releasing Elvis from his Sun Records contract and nominating Colonel Parker his 'sole representative'.

January 17, 1957

Mr. Elvis Presley
Hollywood, California

Dear Mr. Presley:

In consideration and in recognition of your arranging for the
cooperation of Colonel Thomas Parker or his assistant, at our
Studios, during the period of rendition of your services in our
motion picture photoplay tentatively entitled LOVING YOU, and
your cooperation in the preparation and preproduction phases of
our said motion picture photoplay, we hereby agree to pay to you
a bonus of Twenty-five Thousand Dollars ($25,000.00), payable as
follows:

    (a) Five Thousand Dollars ($5,000.00) on January 18, 1957,
        and

    (b) Two Thousand Five Hundred Dollars ($2,500.00) per week
        thereafter for a period of eight (8) weeks.

It is understood that we shall be under no obligation to you or
to Colonel Thomas Parker or his assistant for any services which
may be rendered by them or any expenses incurred by them during
the period of rendition of your services in our said motion
picture photoplay, it being further understood that you shall pay
for such services and such expenses.

It is further understood and agreed that payment to you hereunder
by way of bonus is not intended to and does not vary the terms
and conditions of our employment agreement with you dated April 2,
1956, which is in all respects ratified and confirmed.

If the foregoing correctly sets forth our understanding, please
signify your acceptance at the place indicated below.

Yours very truly,

Hal B. Wallis

ACCEPTED:

Elvis Presley

Joseph H. Hazen

APPROVED:

Colonel Thomas Parker

It was a heady time for the young star. A rare
misstep came when he played a two-week stint in
Las Vegas in late April/early May. Elvis appealed
to a teenage audience who weren't allowed in the
casino lounges, and the adult audiences gave him a
more subdued response than he was used to. But a
matinee show was organized for the teens, and when
he was checking out the other acts on the Strip, Elvis
discovered the song he'd record for his next single,
when he saw Freddy Bell and the Bellboys performing
Big Mama's Thornton's 'Hound Dog' at the Sands.

ABOVE: Contract for
Loving You, 1957, signed
by Hal Wallis, Elvis, and
Colonel Parker.

RIGHT: Elvis' triumphant
homecoming show in
Tupelo on September
26, 1956.

ELVIS PRESLEY PAYROLL & EXPENSE FUND

DATE		PAID TO	AMOUNT		Bank Salary
11-2-56	1	All Star Show, #754,767,782,783,784,794,795,796,797	1,417	98	1700 00
11-2-56	2	Eugene Smith, Sal. w/e 11/3/56 SS. 2.00; WT 16.10	81	90	81. 90
11-5-56	3	First Am. Natl. Bk., Nash., WT Dept. for Oct. & SS.	353	20	353. 20
	4	VOID			
11-6-56	5	Trude Forsher, EP- Cafe De Paris 9/21 -10/1 (Dr. Rm. 6)	17	90	
11-8-56	6	Wm. P. Black ; Sal. w/e 11-10-56 100.00 - WT, 9.20; S.S.	90	80	90. 80
11-8-56	7	W. Scott Moore, Sal., w/e 11/10-56 S.S. it. WT. 11.50	88	50	88. 50
11-10-56	8	D. J. Fontana, Sal. w/e 11-10-56 WT. 16.10	83	90	83. 90
11-8-56	9	Eugene Smith, Sal; W/e 11/10/56 100.00; WT 16.10; SS. 2.00	81	90	81. 90
11-15-56	10	Wm. P. Black, Sal w/e 11/17/56 100.00 WT .9.20	90	80	90. 80
11-15-56	11	W. Scott Moore, Sal. w/e 11/17/56 - 100.00; WT. 11.50	88	50	88. 50
11-15-56	12	D. J. Fontana; Sal. w/e 11/17/56; WT 16.10	83	90	83. 90
11-15-56	13	Eugene Smith Sal w/e 11/17/56; 100.00; S.S. 2.00; WT 16.10	81	90	81. 90
	14	VOID			
11-19-56	15	Cash; Reimburse T.Diskin EPExp. Las Vegas, Nov 9-16,56 Pd.TD	50	00	
11-19-56	16	Cash, Oct. 28 '56; N.Y Sullivan Show, EP Incidental Exp. pd."	155	75	
11-20-56	17	All Star Shows, Hotel Bill Warwick, Moore & Gleaves chg. Col.	39	93	
	18	VOID			
	19	VOID			
	20	VOID			
11-20-56	21	Eugene Smith Sal w/e 11/24/56; 100.00 WT 16.10; SS. 2.00	81	90	81. 90
11-24-56	22	Bill Black; Gas & Oil for limosene Nov. 22-25	100	00	
11-24-56	23	Cash; Adv. to Bitsy Mott for EP Exp. Troy Ohio, Nov. 24	200	00	
	24	Elvis Presley, Cash for purchas of car for Grand parents	2,000	00	
	25	Hotel Seelback, Louis., Ky. Pres. party & Band 11/25 Louis	151	85	
	26	Wm. P. Black, Sal. w/e 11/25; 200.00; WT 25.90	174	10	174 10
	27	W. Scott Moore; Sal W/E 11/25/56; 200.00; S.S.- WT 29.10	170	90	170. 90
	28	D. J. Fontana; Sal. w/e 11/25/56; 200.00 WT 33.70	166	30	166. 30
11-26-56	29	Elvis Presley ; payment towards payment of purchase of car GP	500	00	
11-30-56	30	Hotel Seelback, Rms. 934-36-38; 11/27 Exp. Louisville Ky. EP	10	81	

241850

ABOVE LEFT: Outgoings from the payroll and expenses fund for Elvis from late 1956.

ABOVE: Outside the New Frontier Hotel, Las Vegas, where Elvis played two weeks of shows in April and May 1956.

LEFT: Elvis with former manager Arthur Groom at Loew's State Theater. Elvis' first job was as an usher there.

OPPOSITE: Elvis' triumphant homecoming show in Tupelo on September 26, 1956.

Elvis' recording of 'Hound Dog' would be released that July on what would be his best-selling single (with 'Don't Be Cruel' on the flip side). But it would also land him in hot water, when he first performed it on *The Milton Berle Show* on June 5. His bump-and-grind routine during the song's extended ending outraged more conservative viewers who branded him a menace to young people everywhere. When he appeared on *The Steve Allen Show* a month later, the show's host tried to flip the controversy on its head, putting Elvis in white tie and tails; Elvis looked distinctly uncomfortable, but was fully cooperative. And the ratings that resulted were too good to ignore; Ed Sullivan, who'd previously stated his show wouldn't book Elvis, now booked him for three performances, the first of which was in September — an appearance Elvis fit in between work on his first movie, *Love Me Tender.*

Two triumphant homecoming shows were scheduled for September 26 in at the Mississippi-Alabama Fair and Dairy Show in Tupelo — 11 years after he had made his first public performance at the same event. He received a key to the city from the mayor, while the governor read from a proclamation that acclaimed Elvis as "America's number-one entertainer … [our] own native son." Elvis joked it was one of the few times he hadn't had to sneak into the Fair without paying.

1957 proved to be a less hectic year for Elvis. His live appearances were scaled back, as he concentrated on movie work, making both *Loving You* and *Jailhouse Rock.* He began an association with the legendary songwriting team of Jerry Leiber and Mike Stoller, who'd written 'Hound Dog,' and now contributed songs to both films, including the title numbers. The songwriters were impressed with Elvis' extensive knowledge of music, and when Elvis told them "I'd really like you to write a ballad, a really pretty ballad, for me," the two promptly wrote the song 'Don't' that week — another #1 hit.

Elvis was also adding more musicians to the roster of people he regularly worked with. After his initial RCA sessions, he asked to have the Jordanaires, who'd backed artists like Jim Reeves and Patsy Cline, to be his regular backing vocalists. He also worked for the first time with singer Millie Kirkham in 1957, and her ethereal soprano would grace many of Elvis' recordings. Elvis was very

particular about his work in the studio. "He had a good ear, he had a real good ear," said DJ Fontana. "And he knew what he wanted to hear." Working hard to make the best possible recording gave Elvis' records a distinct sound.

But there were changes looming on the horizon. In December 1957, Elvis received his draft notice. He requested and received a deferment so he could make his next film, *King Creole,* which was filmed from January to March 1958. Elvis worried about the impact his two-year absence would have on his career, but his manager assured him the staggered release of singles and albums over the coming months, as well as

ABOVE: Elvis outside Graceland, during a rare break from his touring schedule.

his new movie, would help keep him in the public eye.

Elvis was inducted into the army on March 24, 1958. He was stationed at Fort Hood in Killeen, Texas. Because soldiers with dependents were allowed to live off base after basic training, Elvis arranged for his legal dependents — his parents — to come to Texas, renting a house where they all could live. During a furlough in June, he also managed to record another five songs, including the future hits 'A Fool Such As I' and 'A Big Hunk O' Love.'

Meanwhile, Gladys Presley had become increasingly unwell. In August, her condition worsened and she returned to Memphis where she was taken into hospital: the diagnosis was hepatitis. Elvis received emergency leave from the army and returned to Memphis himself on August 12. Gladys died two days later, at the age of 46. The emotional toll on Elvis was incalculable, and more than one person close to him observed that he was never quite the same again. As he movingly said later, "It wasn't only like losing a mother, it was like losing a friend, a companion, someone to talk to. I could wake her up any hour of the night if I was worried or troubled about something, well, she'd get up and try to help me." The loss of his mother left an irreplaceable hole in Elvis' life.

He then had to return to his army life. In September, as the soundtrack for *King Creole* was going up the charts (where it would peak at #2), Elvis learned he would be stationed overseas in Germany. He was glad to get away at this emotionally trying time, even as he hoped his manager was right about his career prospects after his army hitch was up.

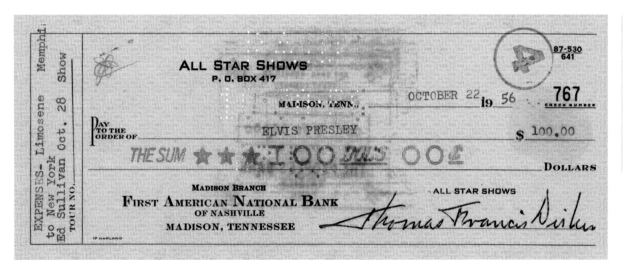

ABOVE and OVERLEAF: 'Heartbreak Hotel' original sheet music, 1956.

LEFT: Check to Elvis to pay for his limousine that took him to *The Ed Sullivan Show*, 1956.

HEARTBREAK HOTEL

By MAE BOREN AXTON, TOMMY DURDEN
and ELVIS PRESLEY

Heart-Break Hotel-2

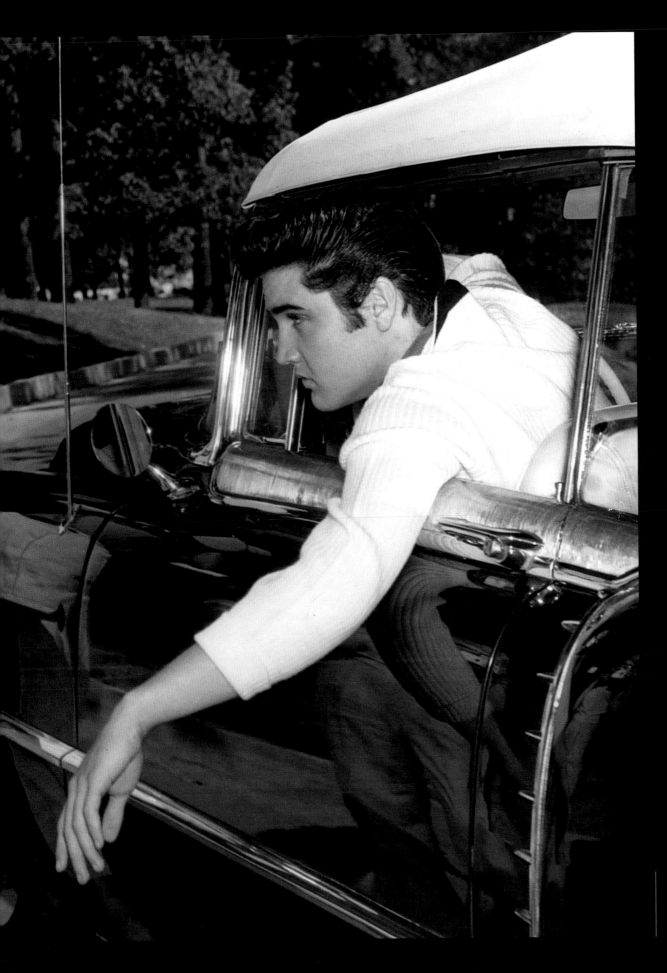

LEFT: Elvis stops to pose for the fans in the driveway of his new home, Graceland, in 1957.

ELVIS PRESLEY

The Elvis Presley *album was an instant classic, starting with its riveting cover shot of Elvis in performance, captured in mid-strum, mouth open in full cry, eyes shut, giving himself over to the moment completely — an image that inspired subsequent tributes on album covers by acts as diverse as the Clash and k.d. lang. The picture had been taken a mere eight months before the album's release, at a July 31, 1955 performance in Tampa, Florida. But how much had changed since then.*

Released: March 1956
Chart position: #1

Most importantly, of course, Elvis was now an RCA recording artist, and the wisdom of that investment was confirmed by the album's initial sales of over 300,000 copies, making it the label's biggest seller to date — at least until the release of the next Elvis record.

Most of the album's dozen songs were recorded in January and February 1956, with a few songs recorded during Elvis' days at Sun. The album gets off to an exciting start with a cover of Carl Perkins' 'Blue Suede Shoes' that's so full of energy it's positively irresistible. Elvis' rocking side is displayed to good effect throughout the album. Ray Charles' 'I Got A Woman' was already a vibrant part of his live show, a number he had great fun with and continued to perform live throughout his career. There's also a frantic romp through Little Richard's 'Tutti Frutti.' You can practically see Elvis' leg jumping in time with the rhythm of 'Just Because,' cut during the Sun days, which also shows off some fine guitar work by Scotty Moore.

But Elvis was capable of far more than simply rocking out. 'One-Sided Love Affair' features a marvelously playful vocal from Elvis, taunting a little bit, teasing a little bit. 'Trying To Get To You,' recorded at Sun, is another mid-tempo number that has one of Elvis' most passionate vocals — just listen to the intensity as his voice goes up an octave during the bridge. Some of that same spirit also comes through in 'I'm Gonna Sit Right Down And Cry (Over You)', a light-hearted number that breezily dismisses the idea of impending heartbreak.

Elvis also got the chance to display his musical versatility through the number of ballads on the album, beginning with the sweet plea of 'I'm Counting On You.' 'I Love You Because,' from the Sun era, features the kind of plaintive, yearning vocals that entranced Elvis' teenage girlfriends back in Memphis before he'd ever stepped into a recording studio. 'I'll Never Let You Go (Little Darlin'),' another Sun track, has a nice twist; though it starts out as a slow number, part way through there's a sudden swing to a light rockabilly tempo, giving the song a more upbeat ending.

And then there's the superlative 'Blue Moon,' cut back at Sun at Elvis' suggestion. Interestingly, though the Richard Rodgers/Lorenz Hart song makes it clear the lonely singer does eventually find love, in Elvis' version these verses are missing, making the song even more melancholy. Elvis' ghostly wailing adds to the ethereal atmosphere of this haunting number.

The album comes to a confident conclusion with 'Money Honey,' which has the kind of insouciance that's on display in 'One-Sided Love Affair.' It's a jaunty, strutting number that places Elvis right in the center of the action, giving the album a bold finish.

At the time of its release, *Elvis Presley* captured attention because of its strong sales and good chart performance (it quickly became Elvis' first #1 album). Its greater important is that it finally gave Elvis a chance to stretch out. Most of his fans had only heard the 'Heartbreak Hotel' single when *Elvis Presley* was released. But the range of material on the album revealed something even more exciting: Elvis was just getting started.

RIGHT: Elvis posing in front of his own cut-out at the New Frontier Hotel, Las Vegas, 1956.

FAR RIGHT: Elvis performing at a concert in Tampa, Florida in 1955.

SILVER SCREEN ELVIS: THE 1950S

The four movies Elvis made during the 1950s featured some of his best work. Elvis was a keen movie fan, and had long dreamed of seeing himself up on the big screen with the other stars. His dreams finally came true in 1956 when he became a full-fledged matinee idol as well as a singing star.

Elvis' film debut was in the Civil War-era drama *Love Me Tender*. Elvis plays the youngest of four siblings, left behind at home while his elder brothers go off to fight the War between the States. After hearing that his older brother, Vance (Richard Egan), has been killed, he marries his brother's sweetheart, Cathy (Debra Paget). After the war, the brothers return — and it turns out Vance is alive, setting up all kind of complications. Elvis had hoped he wouldn't be singing in his movies, but the producers couldn't resist squeezing in a few songs, the best of which was the lovely title number, its melody taken from the Civil War tune 'Aura Lee.'

Loving You, Elvis' first color film, was loosely based on his own rise to fame. Elvis plays Deke Rivers, a truck driver (Elvis' real occupation when he first started recording), who becomes a singing star. Deke's wild shows provoke riots; jealous boyfriends take a swing at him; the authorities are outraged by this newfangled rock 'n' roll stuff. It may be a standard rags-to-riches story, but Elvis' performance brings a real zest and energy to the film. One of the film's highlights is when Elvis sings 'Teddy Bear,' wearing a gorgeous red and white suit designed by Nudie Cohn (who also designed Elvis' famous gold lamé suit). Though Elvis' exuberant performance of 'Got A Lot O' Livin' To Do' toward the film's end, with his parents watching him from the audience, is a close second.

It's back to black-and-white in *Jailhouse Rock*, another dramatic turn for Elvis. He plays Vince Everett, a construction worker who accidentally

While there, he meets an old-time country singer (Mickey Shaughnessy) who gives him the idea to pursue a singing career himself once he's served his time. This results in the best production number of Elvis' career, 'Jailhouse Rock,' which has Elvis and his fellow prisoners dancing their way out of their prison cells; Elvis fine-tuned his dance moves after getting some tips from future *West Side Story* star Russ Tamblyn. In contrast to his first two film roles, Vince isn't completely sweet and innocent; instead, he's ruthless in his efforts to get ahead in the business. Surly Vince also gets off a classic line after he grabs his business partner, Peggy (Judy Tyler) for a kiss, and she admonishes him by saying "How dare you think such cheap tactics would work with me!" "That ain't tactics, honey," Vince replies with studied cool, "that's just the beast in me."

Elvis always cited *King Creole* as his favorite film. The story was based on Harold Robbins' novel *A Stone For Danny Fisher*, though Fisher's profession is changed from a boxer to a singer to better suit Elvis' talents, and the location switched from New York to New Orleans. It was the perfect musical setting, as seen from the very first number, 'Crawfish,' a duet Elvis does with a street vendor, through terrific performances of 'Trouble,' 'Hard Headed Woman,' and the title song. Elvis also shines dramatically, torn between an ineffectual father (Dean Jagger) and a heavyweight gangster (Walter Matthau), as well two love interests, one sultry (Carolyn Jones) and one sweet (Dolores Hart).

Elvis not only made classic rock 'n' roll records in the 1950s; he made classic rock 'n' roll movies

NOW **NOW**

ARS GRATIA ARTIS

M-G-M

Presents

ELVIS PRESLEY
IN JAILHOUSE ROCK

Co-starring **JUDY TYLER**

With **MICKEY SHAUGHNESSY**
DEAN JONES **JENNIFER HOLDEN**

Screen Play by **GUY TROSPER**

in

CINEMASCOPE . . . AN AVON PRODUCTION

Directed by **RICHARD THORPE** Produced by **PANDRO S. BERMAN**

HEAR
RCA VICTOR'S

ELVIS PRESLEY
Sing Title Song
"JAILHOUSE ROCK"
AND OTHER SONG HITS!

OPPOSITE: Elvis casts a shadow in the classic outfit he wore during the 'Teddy Bear' number in *Loving You*.

ABOVE LEFT: A publicity shot from *Love Me Tender*.

ABOVE RIGHT: Elvis wore this sweater when he performed the number 'You're So Square' in *Jailhouse Rock*.

LEFT: Movie poster for *Jailhouse Rock*, 1957.

ELVIS

Elvis capped one of the most successful years in Elvis' career. Another chart-topping album, it achieved record sales for RCA — with initial orders of close to half a million copies, it easily outsold its predecessor. And it was another winning mix of rock 'n' roll, country, ballads and rhythm & blues, once again confirming the musical versatility of America's new rock 'n' roll star.

Most of the *Elvis* album was recorded over three fruitful days in September 1956, sandwiched in between work on the first of Elvis' movies, *Love Me Tender*. He also found the time to record his next single, 'Too Much'/'Playing For Keeps,' at the sessions. Elvis tackled three Little Richard numbers, one of which, 'Rip It Up,' became the album's lead off track, getting the record off to a lively start. 'Long Tall Sally' and 'Ready Teddy' were equally ebullient, both numbers also being live favorites for Elvis, and readily conveying his boundless energy.

'When My Blue Moon Turns To Gold Again' harkened back to the country swing of Elvis' Sun sessions, smartened up by the crisp backing vocals of The Jordanaires, who'd been working as Elvis' accompanying vocalists since June. 'Paralyzed' was another pleasant pop tune from the pen of Otis Blackwell, who'd previously given Elvis a big hit with 'Don't Be Cruel.' 'Anyplace Is Paradise' has an engaging, laidback delivery that also goes down nicely.

Having first made his name with Arthur "Big Boy" Crudup's 'That's All Right,' Elvis dug into the bluesman's repertoire again during the *Elvis* sessions, coming up trumps with 'So Glad You're Mine,' which Elvis delivered as a slinky blues. Jerry Leiber and Mike Stoller's 'Love Me' had started out as a country song, but Elvis takes it down the bluesy side of the street, with a voice that dips down low, then soars aloft, nicely cushioned by the backing vocals of the Jordanaires, who come together with Elvis on the last line. Elvis might have made his name in rock 'n' roll, but the slower

numbers showed how expressive a singer he really could be.

As you'd expect, Elvis puts his heart and soul into the album's ballads. 'First In Line' features a lovely, expressive vocal, while the song as a whole has a touch of doo-wop. The somber 'How's The World Treating You' has another sensitive vocal, standing out even more against the muted musical backdrop.

'Old Shep' is particularly interesting. It's the song Elvis performed in his very first public performance at the Mississippi-Alabama Fair in 1945 when he was 10 years old. It was the kind of song that could be overly sentimental, but Elvis plays it straight, delivering an earnest, heartfelt vocal that can bring tears to your eyes. It's not quite what the attendees at the Fair would have heard, but it clearly demonstrates that Elvis understood what a powerful emotional impact a song could make.

Elvis had tried recording 'How Do You Think I Feel' — previously recorded by Jimmie Rodgers Snow — during his Sun days, although no takes survive. This time, he finally managed to produce a version he liked; a nice slice of country-pop that closes the album.

Released just in time for the Christmas holidays, *Elvis* was a welcome present for the fans.

Interestingly, *Elvis* would be his last new studio album until *Elvis Is Back*, released in 1960. Most of his albums over the next few years would be soundtracks, interspersed with Christmas and Greatest Hits collections. For any connoisseur of popular music, the albums *Elvis Presley* and *Elvis* stand together as superb documents of the early Elvis in his prime.

Released: October 1956
Chart position: #1

RIGHT: Caught with hips in mid-swing during Elvis' October 28, 1956 performance on *The Ed Sullivan Show*.

OVERLEAF LEFT: A soulful moment from a 1950s performance.

OVERLEAF RIGHT: Elvis takes delivery of a console TV set from RCA, in appreciation for the record sales he achieved for the company, in the spring of 1960.

Elvis Presley

ELVIS SINGS CHRISTMAS

Only Elvis could open his Christmas album with a song that has Santa Claus not in his sleigh but driving a "big black Cadillac." Elvis' Christmas Album *had its share of traditional carols — 'O Little Town of Bethlehem,' 'Silent Night') — and other religious numbers, such as 'Peace in the Valley,' 'Take My Hand, Precious Lord,' 'It Is No Secret,' and 'I Believe,' released earlier that year on the EP* Peace In The Valley. *But there were also definite touches of rock 'n' roll and R&B thrown into the mixture.*

ELVIS' CHRISTMAS ALBUM
Released: October 1957
Chart position: #1

Such as in that opening song, 'Santa Claus Is Back In Town,' a playful, bluesy number written for Elvis by Jerry Leiber and Mike Stoller, that makes Santa sound like the hippest cat on the block. 'Blue Christmas' had previously been recorded by other acts (Ernest Tubb, Hugo Winterhalter and His Orchestra, and Russ Morgan and His Orchestra all had hits with the song), but Elvis put his own vocal spin on it, amping up the blues quotient, and so inhabiting the number it's now primarily associated with him.

He also took on one of the most popular Christmas songs of all time: 'White Christmas.' Elvis' smooth rendition took some inspiration from the Drifters' 1954 version, but Elvis slowed down the tempo, giving a touch of dreaminess to the Christmas classic. The album also featured a poignant version of 'I'll Be Home For Christmas,' the lighter pop of 'Santa Bring My Baby Back (To Me)' and a bopping rendition of Gene Autry's 'Here Comes Santa Claus.' Although there was some controversy on release of the album — composer Irving Berlin took exception to Elvis' version of 'White Christmas' — *Elvis' Christmas Album*, packaged in a deluxe gatefold sleeve, quickly went to the top of the charts.

Elvis' next Christmas release was the single 'If Every Day Could Be Like Christmas,' written by his friend Red West and released in November 1966. In 1971, it was decided that the time was right for a new collection of Christmas songs, and during the sessions, a Christmas tree with wrapped presents was set up to help get Elvis in the proper festive

mood. The standout track is 'Merry Christmas Baby,' a steamy slice of R&B that goes on for nearly six minutes, Elvis' rich vocal matched by a great guitar break from James Burton.

Most of the songs on the album were from the modern era. Red West came up with another holiday tune, the nostalgic 'Holly Leaves And Christmas Trees.' A number of the songs had a bittersweet separated-at-the-holidays theme. In 'I'll Be Home On Christmas Day,' Elvis seals his promise to return with a nice soulful vocal. There's a pleasant country flavor to 'It Won't Seem Like Christmas (Without You),' and the hopes in 'If I Get Home On Christmas Day' soar as high as the delicate backing vocals.

The dynamics of 'The Wonderful World Of Christmas' are especially pleasing, with the quieter verses rising to a stirring ringing chorus, replete with bells. Elvis also conjures up a lovely mellow mood in 'On A Snowy Christmas Night.' You'll also find some traditional carols ('O Come, All Ye Faithful,' 'The First Noel'), and a few modern favorites (a jaunty 'Winter Wonderland,' and a warm 'Silver Bells,' which closes the album). Technically, *Elvis Sings The Wonderful World Of Christmas* never charted although it was very popular upon its release in the early 1970s, and subsequently.

Today, you can find all of Elvis' Christmas songs packaged in collections such as *White Christmas* (2000), *Christmas Peace* (2003) and *Elvis Christmas* (2006).

ELVIS SINGS THE WONDERFUL WORLD OF CHRISTMAS
Released: October 1971

RIGHT: Whatever else he did during the year, Elvis always made sure to spend the Christmas holidays at Graceland.

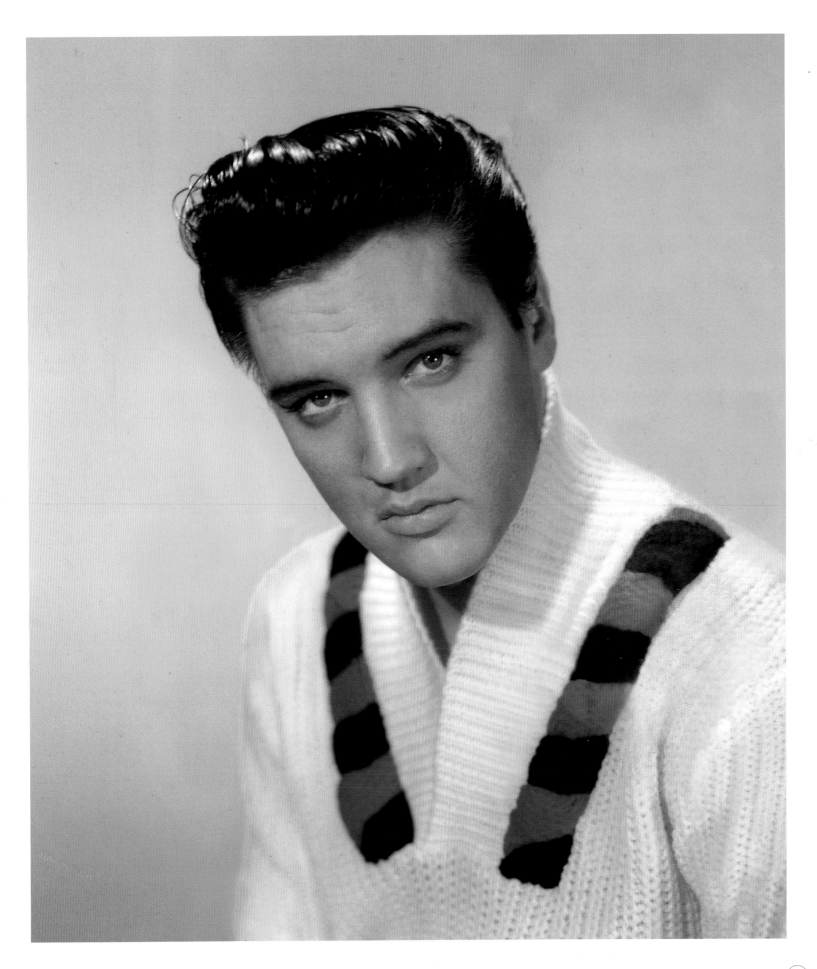

SOLDIER BOY

Elvis spent 18 months of his time in the army in Germany. After basic training in Texas he shipped out from Brooklyn on September 22, 1958; excerpts from the press conference held before his departure were quickly released on the record Elvis Sails. *The troop ship arrived in Bremerhaven on October 1 from where Elvis traveled to his army base in Friedberg, 200 miles north of Frankfurt. Elvis was a member of the 32nd Tank Battalion, Third Armored Division, serving as a jeep driver for his commanding officers. He would also spend a good deal of time out in the field on maneuvers, all of which helped keep him out of the public eye.*

Once again, Elvis was allowed to live off base with his father and grandmother. Vernon and Minnie Mae, along with his friends Red West and Lamar Fike, arrived in Germany shortly after Elvis, and for a time they lived in hotels. Eventually, desiring more room and greater privacy, Elvis rented a house located at 14 Goethestrasse, Bad Nauheim, in January 1959. He would live there until he departed for Memphis in March of 1960.

Elvis was soon at home in his new surroundings. Evenings were spent at the movies, or gathered around the piano at 14 Geothestrasse for informal sing-alongs (some of these sessions were taped and later released on collections like *The Home Recordings*). Elvis headed up a team that played touch football every weekend. A secretary was hired to answer fan mail, and a sign posted outside informed passers-by that Elvis would sign autographs every evening between 7:30 and 8 pm — something he regularly did throughout his stay, to the delight of the fans who maintained a constant vigil outside his home in the hopes of seeing him.

Elvis also met a number of people during his time abroad who would go on to become key members of his inner circle. He first met Charlie Hodge when traveling on the troop train to Brooklyn. Charlie was a performer himself, having sung with the Foggy River Boys, and it turned out that he and Elvis had a number of common acquaintances. The pair spent much time singing and harmonizing together, a role Charlie would continue to play in Elvis' life. A mutual friend introduced another soldier, Joe Esposito, to Elvis. Joe had a natural flair for organization, and during a trip to Paris in early 1960, he'd been put in charge of looking after the money and keeping track of the receipts. As a result of his efficiency, he was asked to work for Elvis when they left the army. Elvis had found a loyal worker and a lifelong friend.

Then, on September 13, 1959, Elvis met 14-year-old Priscilla Beaulieu, who had been brought to 14 Geothestrasse by a mutual friend. Priscilla was the daughter of an Air Force captain, and had arrived in Germany just the month before. Elvis was especially taken with Priscilla, and she became a regular visitor to his home, where she spent hours talking to him, or sitting by his side as he played the piano.

"People were expecting me to goof up," Elvis said in an interview with Armed Forces Radio of his military experience. "They thought I couldn't take it, and I was determined to go to any limits to prove otherwise." And so he had. On March 5, 1960, Elvis' active duty with the army was over. He would serve another four years in the army reserves and be discharged from the army in March 1964. By the time he left Germany he had been promoted to sergeant, and he left his combat jacket with Priscilla, promising they would see each other again. But now, it was time to get back to work.

RIGHT: The army frequently sent Elvis on maneuvers to keep him at arm's length from fans.

COLONEL TOM PARKER
% RCA VICTOR RECORDS
155 E. 24TH STREET
NEW YORK, NEW YORK

19.1.59
12⁴⁰ h

DEAR COLONEL:

WHILE YOU ARE IN NEW YORK ON BUSINESS WOULD APPRECIATE IF YOU CAN
WORK OUT SOMETHING WITH RCA VICTOR FOLKS WHERE I CAN GET A MESSAGE
TO THE FANS. I WANT TO BE ABLE TO THANK THEM NOT ONLY FOR BUYING
MY RECORDS AND FOR THEIR LOYALTY TO ME BUT ALSO FOR THE HELP
THEY HAVE GIVEN ME IN DECIDING THE KIND OF SONGS TO SING FOR IN
TALKING WITH THEM AND READING THEIR LETTERS I WAS ABLE TO GET SOME
IDEA OF WHAT THEY LIKED. I'M DEEPLY GRATEFUL TO THEM AND I WANT
THEM TO KNOW IT. WHEN I'M OUT OF THE ARMY AND RECORDING AGAIN I
WILL ALWAYS LISTEN TO THEIR IDEAS JUST AS I DID BEFORE. I JUST
WANTED TO LET MY FANS KNOW HOW I FEEL.

                              SINCERELY,

                              ELVIS

U.S. GOVERNMENT OPERATOR'S PERMIT		PERMIT NO.
DEPARTMENT OF DEFENSE AR 600-55		0213

NAME OF OPERATOR			DATE ISSUED	EXPIRATION DATE
Presley, Elvis A			11 Aug 58	10 Aug 6

SEX	RACE	AGE	HEIGHT	WEIGHT	COLOR OF HAIR	COLOR OF EYES
Male	Cau	23	6'	180	Brown	Blue

The holder of this permit is qualified to operate U. S. Government vehicles
and/or equipment specified subject to the restrictions set forth on the reverse
hereof.

SIGNATURE OF ISSUING OFFICIAL	TITLE
Max R Griff	CWO-3 USA

NAME AND LOCATION OF ISSUING UNIT Hq 2d Med Tk Bn (Patton)
37th Armor, 2d AD, Fort Hood, Texas

NOT TRANSFERABLE
Permit must be carried at all times when operating Government vehicles.

SIGNATURE OF OPERATOR (*Not valid until signed*)
Elvis Presley

D FORM 313, 1 AUG 50 REPLACES WD AGO FORM 9-74, 1 AUG 48, WHICH MAY BE USED.

ABOVE: Typed letter to Colonel Parker from Elvis, January 19, 1959.

LEFT: Elvis' Government Operator's Permit, allowing him to drive trucks for the army, 1958.

RIGHT: His army hitch done, Elvis greets his stateside fans with a huge smile when he arrives at McGuire Air Force Base, New Jersey on March 3, 1960

MOVIE MAKING, MUSIC MAKING

Once freed of his military obligations, Elvis' first task was to record a new single. Although there was a little tension in the air when Elvis returned to RCA's Nashville studio on March 20, 1960, he was also surrounded by friends and familiar faces — Scotty Moore and DJ Fontana were present, as were the Jordanaires — all of whom helped put him at ease. Over the course of the evening he recorded two songs for his next single, the poppy 'Stuck On You' and the ballad (with its hint of doo wop) 'Fame And Fortune,' as well as four other tracks intended for his next album. Within 48 hours, 'Stuck On You' was in the shops, on its way to the Number One spot.

By then, Elvis was in Miami, preparing for his guest appearance on the television special *The Frank Sinatra Timex Show: Welcome Home Elvis*. Elvis sang both sides of his new single, and also engaged in a "song swap" with his host, Frank singing Elvis' 'Love Me Tender,' and Elvis taking on Frank's 'Witchcraft.'

Frank's daughter, Nancy, would also make her professional debut on the show; on looking at Elvis during the opening number, she sings "I may pass out!" Nancy would later co-star with Elvis on the film *Speedway*.

The following month Elvis completed his next album, the appropriately titled *Elvis Is Back!*, then began work on his first post-army film, *G.I. Blues*. From this point, film work began to dominate his career; in 1960 Elvis would shoot *Flaming Star* and *Wild In The Country*, along with *G.I. Blues*. There was a practical side to this career direction. More people could see a film that could ever hope to see Elvis perform live. And the film would naturally promote the soundtrack, while the soundtrack would promote the film — a neat piece of cross-promotion.

It wasn't until 1961 that Elvis returned to live performance. Two charity concerts were held in Memphis on February 25 at the Ellis Auditorium — the same venue where Elvis had seen so many all-night gospel shows — and another benefit concert on March 25 in Honolulu, a fundraiser for the *U.S.S.*

Arizona memorial. Ray Walker of the Jordanaires recalled the shows as crackling with excitement. "He just had kind of an effervescence about him," he said. "He would do some unexpected things and do them so well we'd forget to come in." But they were also the last live performances Elvis would make for another seven years.

Elvis was now making movies almost full time, usually three films a year: *Blue Hawaii, Follow That Dream,* and *Kid Galahad* in 1961; *Girls! Girls! Girls!* and *It Happened At The World's Fair* in 1962; *Fun In Acapulco, Viva Las Vegas,* and *Kissin' Cousins* in 1963; *Roustabout, Girl Happy,* and *Tickle Me* in 1964; *Harum Scarum, Frankie And Johnny,* and *Paradise, Hawaiian Style* in 1965; *Spinout, Double Trouble,* and *Easy Come, Easy Go* in 1966. Most of the soundtracks reached the Top 20, generally accompanied by a hit single: 'Can't Help Falling In Love' from *Blue Hawaii,* 'Return to Sender' from *Girls! Girls! Girls!,* 'Bossa Nova Baby' from *Fun In Acapulco.* The release of the films was often tied to the school holidays — spring break, summer break, Christmas break — when Elvis' fan base would have more free time to see the movies.

But Elvis was no longer just a teen idol. He had grown up, as his new musical direction revealed. Songs like 'It's Now Or Never' and 'Are You Lonesome Tonight?' displayed a greater vocal depth than a straight out rocker like 'Hound Dog' or 'Jailhouse Rock.' 'There's Always Me' (on 1961's

RIGHT: It was art imitating life when Elvis, though a civilian, found himself back in fatigues for his first post-army film, *G. I. Blues.*

THE PACIFIC WAR MEMORIAL COMMISSION

proudly presents **ELVIS PRESLEY**
IN PERSON

★ WITH ALL-STAR CAST ★

AT BLOCH ARENA **PEARL HARBOR**
Saturday, March 25th 8:30 p.m.
Doors Open 7:15

MAIN FLOOR
39

$100 SECTION

OPPOSITE: A sophisticated shot of Elvis as he appeared in *Girls! Girls! Girls!*

ABOVE: Ticket to the Pearl Harbor memorial concert at the Bloch Arena, March 25, 1961.

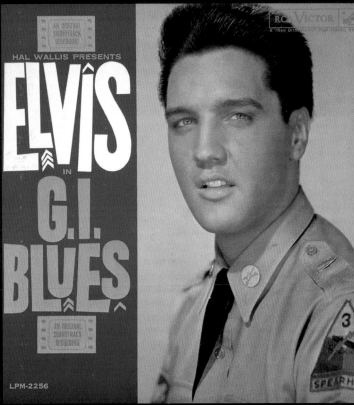

On the check:
E. A. PRESLEY
3764 HIGHWAY 51, SOUTH
MEMPHIS, TENNESSEE

910

26-1
840

PAID Feb 14 1964

721

PAY TO THE ORDER OF William Morris Agency Inc $55,000.00

Fifty Five Thousand and 00/xx DOLLARS

NATIONAL BANK OF COMMERCE
MEMPHIS, TENNESSEE

E. A. PRESLEY

E. A. Presley

⑈0840⑈0001⑈ 0⑈⑈ ⑈43875⑈

(handwritten left side: To St Jude Hospital, Memphis Tenn for Purchase of Potomac. Confinscatkuat # 1130)

Something For Everybody) and 'Suspicion' (on 1962's *Pot Luck*), exhibited a similar flair for the dramatic. In the early 1960s, Elvis didn't often record the kind of rock 'n' roll that he had the previous decade, although he make two passes at Chuck Berry's 'Memphis, Tennessee' in 1963 and 1965; the latter version was released first, appearing on the 1965 album *Elvis For Everyone*. He was more often drawn to the blues — songs such as the sly 'Put The Blame On Me,' which appeared on *Something For Everybody*. And he was always partial to ballads. One of the highlights of this period was 'That's Someone You Never Forget,' a mesmerizing number written by his friend Red West, with Elvis receiving a co-writing credit for coming up with the title and the song's primary theme. The song was open to interpretation; it could have been addressed to a romantic partner, or perhaps another loved one. Was Elvis, people wondered, thinking about his mother? The song was released on 1962's *Pot Luck*.

In 1960, Elvis released his first religious album, *His Hand In Mine*. 'Crying in the Chapel,' a song recorded at the session which hadn't been included on the album, was finally released in 1965, and reached #3, his highest charting single in two years.

Due to the album's success, immediate plans were made to record another religious album in May 1966. The May sessions, and the June date that followed, would prove to be very important to Elvis' career for several reasons. First, Elvis was working with a new producer, Felton Jarvis. Felton had actually seen Elvis perform back in 1955, and went on to record an Elvis tribute record ('Don't Knock Elvis'), later producing acts like Gladys Knight and The Pips, Willie Nelson,

and Tommy Roe's chart-topping hit, 'Sheila.' Elvis' previous producer, Chet Atkins, felt that Elvis and Felton would hit it off — and they did. Felton would be intensely loyal remaining as his producer for the rest of Elvis' career.

The sessions also gave Elvis the opportunity to stretch out musically. There was no question he was excited about being able to record the gospel music he most loved. But there were also other numbers recorded in May and June, some for single release, others to fill out the *Spinout* soundtrack, that featured some of his best work. 'Indescribably Blue' (released as a single) was a lovely ballad, while the songs recorded as bonus tracks on *Spinout* were excellent examples of Elvis' superlative vocal skills. 'Down in the Alley' was a terrific, gritty blues. 'I'll Remember You,' was a song of haunting beauty. And his version of Bob Dylan's 'Tomorrow Is A Long Time' was remarkable. At almost five and a half minutes, it's one of Elvis' longest songs and the simple arrangement nicely contrasts his delicate vocal with a backing consisting solely of acoustic guitar, bass, and tambourine. It was a superlative piece of work that Dylan himself later cited as one of his favorite cover versions. When Elvis was matched with the right material, there was no one who could surpass him.

Finally, the religious album resulting from the sessions, *How Great Thou Art*, gave Elvis his first Grammy win, after nine previous nominations, taking home the award for Best Sacred Performance. It was a great honor that renewed Elvis' faith in his talent. He had conquered the recording industry in the 1950s. He had become a major film star in the 1960s. Now he was ready for a new challenge.

ABOVE: Check to the William Morris Agency for the purchase of the *Potomac*, 1964.

RIGHT: A relaxed Elvis, on the set of *Blue Hawaii*, 1961.

SILVER SCREEN ELVIS: THE 1960s

Elvis made 27 movies between 1960 and 1969. Most were light comedies — G.I. Blues, his first post-army film, setting the template. Elvis usually portrayed a young man in some rugged profession — racing car driver, dust-crop pilot, deep sea diver — who was both eager to better his position and win the hand of his love interest. Naturally, he has little difficulty in attaining both goals by the final reel. The fun is in watching him get there.

This formula was perfected in *Blue Hawaii*, Elvis most successful film (leading to two more cinematic excursions to the islands, *Girls! Girls! Girls!* and *Paradise, Hawaiian Style*). *Blue Hawaii* introduced 'Can't Help Falling In Love' into Elvis' repertoire, where it quickly became one of his signature songs; the single reached #2, and from 1969 on, the song regularly closed his live concert performances. The film's soundtrack was just as successful, topping the charts for 20 weeks — the longest time any of Elvis' albums spent at the Number One spot.

The soundtracks for *G.I. Blues* and *Roustabout* also went to #1, while nine other soundtracks for Elvis' films reached the Top 20. And you'll find a number of memorable songs in Elvis' movies. 'Wooden Heart' in *G.I. Blues*. 'King Of The Whole Wide World' in *Kid Galahad*. 'Return To Sender' in *Girls! Girls! Girls!* 'One Broken Heart For Sale' in *It Happened At The World's Fair*. 'Bossa Nova Baby' in *Fun In Acapulco*. 'Little Egypt' in *Roustabout*. The 'Down By The Riverside'/'When The Saints Go Marching In' medley in *Frankie And Johnny*. 'Let Yourself Go' in *Speedway*. 'Swing Down Sweet Chariot' in *The Trouble With Girls (And How To Get Into It)*. 'Rubberneckin'' in *Change Of Habit*. 'Viva Las Vegas' was one of the best title songs of any of Elvis' films, with the theme song for 'Follow That Dream' another strong contender.

A good co-star always brought out the best in Elvis. The most exciting co-star Elvis was paired with in the 1960s was undoubtedly Ann-Margret (who had previously appeared in the film version of the Broadway musical *Bye Bye Birdie*, about an Elvis-type singer, Conrad Birdie, who is drafted into the army).

The two stars positively sizzle in their dance numbers together, 'C'mon Everybody' and 'What'd I Say,' while also deftly handling the witty comedy of the song 'The Lady Loves Me' (another stellar moment in the film is Elvis' introspective number, 'I Need Somebody To Lean On').

Nancy Sinatra was another good foil for Elvis in *Speedway*, even getting her own number in the film, 'Your Groovy Self,' written by Lee Hazlewood, who'd also written Nancy's signature song 'These Boots Are Made For Walkin'.' Two of Elvis' other glamorous leading ladies were Juliet Prowse (a nightclub dancer in *G.I. Blues*) and Ursula Andress (a hotel director in *Fun In Acapulco*).

Elvis was especially fond of Shelley Fabares, who co-starred in no fewer than three of Elvis' movies. In *Girl Happy* she plays a college student on spring break, with Elvis as the chaperone hired by her father to look after her; the film's high point is the big production number for 'Do The Clam,' which has Elvis and Shelley dancing away on the beach. In *Spinout*, Shelley plays an heiress with an eye for Elvis; he nonetheless manages to not succumb to her charms. *Clambake* is an updated take on *The Prince and the Pauper* story, with Shelley yearning to marry a rich man, not knowing that Elvis is a millionaire in disguise. The two had the kind of friendly camaraderie that makes it easy to see why she was one of Elvis' favorite co-stars.

Not every Elvis film was a light comedy. His strongest dramatic performance in the '60s was in *Wild In The Country*, playing a hot-tempered rebel who learns to overcome his demons and pursue a writing career. The literate script, by noted writer Clifford Odets, had Elvis caught between three

RIGHT: *Charro!* was the only Elvis movie to feature just one musical number — the title song.

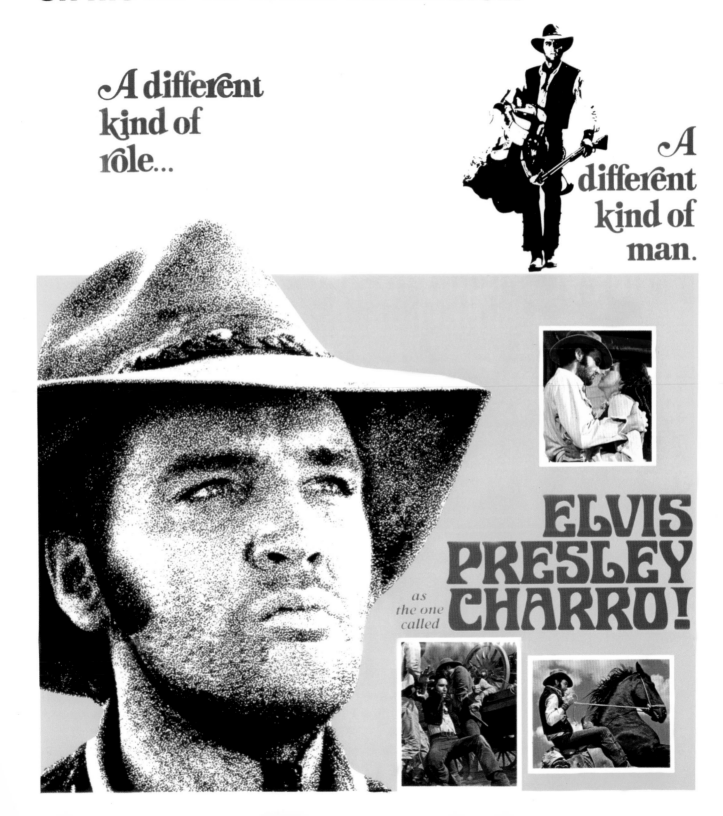

ON HIS NECK HE WORE THE BRAND OF A KILLER.
ON HIS HIP HE WORE VENGEANCE.

A different kind of role...

A different kind of man.

ELVIS PRESLEY CHARRO!

as the one called

women: Millie Perkins, Tuesday Weld, and Hope Lange. *Change Of Habit* was another down to earth drama, with Elvis as a doctor working at a free clinic in a poor neighborhood. He takes a shine to Mary Tyler Moore, one of the three volunteers who turn up to work at his clinic, not knowing they're nuns; unusually, the film leaves Mary's dilemma unresolved, and we never learn if she chooses Elvis or decides to remain a nun. Elvis got to do his own Spaghetti Western in *Charro!*, the only Elvis movie to feature a single number: the title song. *Flaming Star* gave him another challenging role, playing the son of a white man and Native American woman, torn between two cultures in 19th-century America.

Some big names turned up in Elvis' movies. Barbara Stanwyck plays a tough carnival owner in *Roustabout*. Elsa Lanchester, the original 'Bride of Frankenstein,' sings a zany duet with Elvis ('Yoga Is As Yoga Does') in *Easy Come, Easy Go*. Singing star Rudy Vallee (who enjoyed Elvis-like success as a singer in the 1930s) plays a magazine editor in *Live A Little, Love A Little*. *Batman* villain "The Penguin" — Burgess Meredith — plays Elvis' father in *Stay Away Joe*. John Carradine and Vincent Price make brief, comedic appearances in *The Trouble With Girls* (which also featured Dabney Coleman in one of his first film roles).

It's also fun to spot well-known performers just getting started in the business. Prior to his fame as an action star, Charles Bronson taught Elvis how to box in *Kid Galahad*. The same film also features future *Mary Tyler Moore/Lou Grant* star Ed Asner in a small role. A pre-*I Dream Of Jeannie* Barbara Eden plays the fiancé of Elvis' brother in *Flaming Star*. An 11-year-old Kurt Russell is seen kicking Elvis in the shin in *It Happened At The World's Fair*; in a neat twist, Russell would go on to play the King himself in the 1979 television film *Elvis*. Elvis' buddies frequently had small roles in his films (often in the fight scenes), and his father Vernon makes a cameo in *Live A Little, Love A Little*.

The movies Elvis made in the 1960s helped establish him as one of the top box office draws of the decade; as one of his producers, Hal Wallis, stated, "A Presley picture is the only sure thing in Hollywood." There were other payoffs as well. *Tickle Me*, in which Elvis played a hired hand at an all-female dude ranch/health spa, became the third highest grossing film in the history of the studio, Allied Artists, saving the studio from bankruptcy. And then there was the Mac Davis number 'A Little Less Conversation,' from the film *Live A Little, Love A Little*. Elvis plays a fashion photographer pursued by an eccentric woman in the film, and sang the song during a party sequence. Twenty-four years later, a dance remix of the song was used in a Nike commercial for that year's soccer World Cup. it proved so popular that the song was released as a single, topping the charts in over 20 countries, including *Billboard*'s Singles Sales charts. All these years later, Elvis' movies continue to surprise us.

ELVIS IS BACK!

The title was as bold as it was hopeful. Elvis Is Back! *not only announced where Elvis was — back from his military service, back in America, back in Memphis — but also where he hoped to be; back on top in the music business.*

Released: April 1960
Chart position: #2

Elvis wasted no time in getting back in the game. Fifteen days after he was mustered out of active duty in the army he entered the studio to record his first new tracks in almost two years. Three songs would appear on *Elvis Is Back!*, but the bulk of the work was recorded in an astonishing 12 hour session on April 3–4, 1960, where Elvis laid down a remarkable 12 tracks.

The final album showed how much Elvis had grown as a vocalist. There was a new confidence evident from the opening bars of 'Make Me Know It,' another pop delight by Otis Blackwell that Elvis handles with breezy aplomb. Next up is a sharp turn into far more sultry territory with Elvis' smoky rendition of 'Fever,' a stripped down arrangement that features only bass and congas, making Elvis sound like he's right there in the room with you. 'The Girl Of My Best Friend' was more typical of some of the light pop numbers of Elvis' pre-army period, but Elvis was now leaning more toward the ballads he had always loved. He'd recorded 'Are You Lonesome Tonight?' for single release during the session, and 'I Will Be Home Again' was in a similarly expressive vein, featuring a nice harmony vocal by Charlie Hodge, whom he'd met in the army, and who would provide similar services throughout Elvis' career.

Then there was another shift in musical mood to the smooth rockin' 'Dirty, Dirty Feeling,' from the Jerry Leiber/Mike Stoller team, and originally a contender for the *King Creole* soundtrack. Side one of the original album closed with the yearning 'Thrill of Your Love'; in just six songs, Elvis gave a nod to his past and showed the way ahead. No longer a raw, unvarnished kid, he had the kind of vocal command that allowed him to tackle any musical style.

'Soldier Boy' was an obvious inclusion given Elvis' recent service (indeed, the album's gatefold sleeve featured "bonus snapshots" of Elvis in uniform). The remaining tracks feature Elvis at his gritty, playful

best. Just listen to the teasing twists in his vocal delivery on 'Such A Night,' the drums providing a nice rolling conclusion to the number. He strolls through the blues of 'It Feels So Right' as if he's got all the time in world, moving on up to the high notes with deceptive ease. 'The Girl Next Door Went A' Walking' has a propulsive energy that carries you along like a swiftly moving stream. 'Like A Baby' was the kind of vocal workout Elvis would specialize in, with a quiet beginning leading to a dramatic vocal that soared above the mere mortals left below. And if 'It Feels So Right' showed his allegiance to the blues, it was topped by his performance on the album's closing track, Lowell Fulson's 'Reconsider Baby.' Bolstered by Homer "Boots" Randolph's wailing saxophone solo, Elvis turned in a masterful vocal — intense, gutsy, and just the right amount of no-nonsense attitude (he also played rhythm guitar on the track as well).

Relaunching his musical career after a two year break offered Elvis the opportunity to go in any number of different directions. His choice was typically Elvis — he chose to display not just one, but all of his musical strengths. It's this versatility that makes *Elvis Is Back!* a truly classic album.

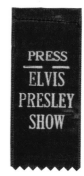

LEFT: Elvis was back to making records within a month of leaving the army.

RIGHT: Elvis' first post-army concert, February 25, 1961 at the Ellis Auditorium in Memphis.

THE COMEBACK

Between 1967 and 1969, Elvis experienced many changes in both his life and his career. Some of those changes were highly personal — he got married and became a father. He had stayed in touch with Priscilla Beaulieu, the teenager he'd met when he was stationed in Germany. In June 1962, Priscilla visited Elvis when he was in Los Angeles, spending Christmas with him in Memphis that same year. In March 1963, Elvis arranged for Priscilla to move to Memphis to be with him; she stayed with his father Vernon, who, with his new wife Dee, lived just around the corner from Graceland.

In December 1966, Elvis proposed marriage. On May 1, 1967, just after Elvis had completed work on Clambake, the wedding party flew to Las Vegas, where Elvis and Priscilla were married at the Aladdin Hotel, with a press conference held after the ceremony, followed by a lavish buffet. Later that month, the newlyweds hosted what Priscilla called a "more comfortable and relaxed" reception for their friends in Memphis.

When Priscilla told Elvis she was pregnant, Elvis was thrilled, passing out cigars on the set of his latest film, *Speedway*, and telling reporters, "This is the greatest thing that has ever happened to me." The couple's daughter, Lisa Marie Presley, was born on May 1, 1968, in Memphis. Elvis was filled with pride, proclaiming to one friend, "She's a little miracle."

Film work continued, on the same steady schedule: in addition to *Clambake* and *Speedway*, the film *Stay Away, Joe* was also made in 1967, and *Live A Little, Love A Little, Charro!*, and *The Trouble With Girls (And How To Get Into It)* were made in 1968. But there were some changes afoot. The films were no longer performing as strongly at the box office: a change of direction was needed. *Speedway* was the last Elvis film accompanied by a soundtrack album; subsequent films would feature far fewer songs. And there were other modern touches; *Speedway* had a groovy, mod club setting, *Live A Little, Love A Little* featured a trippy dream sequence, and *The Trouble With Girls* was an ensemble film, similar to the approach Robert Altman would use in films like *Nashville*.

Elvis was more excited about the new musical directions he was pursuing. At a September 1967

RIGHT: A denim and leather-clad Elvis showed a more down-to-earth image.

BELOW: An Elvis-signed check, 1966. It was payment for a car that Elvis purchased for a co-star.

recording session, he wanted to record Jerry Reed's 'Guitar Man,' and, in order to get the same guitar sound as on Jerry's record, arranged to bring him to the session. Jerry's presence immediately livened things up, and his nimble-fingered guitar work brought a welcome jolt of energy to the session. Elvis had such a good time laying down his vocal, he occasionally segued into Ray Charles' 'What'd I Say' at the end of a take. It was, Jerry later recalled, "One of those rare moments in your life you never forget."

They had just as good a time with Jimmy Reed's 'Big Boss Man,' both it and 'Guitar Man' standing as prime examples of the genre of country rock that Elvis fit into quite naturally. And Elvis was always game for a bluesy spin on a song like 'Hi-Heel Sneakers.' The same lively spirit was there at the next session Jerry Reed attended in January 1968, when Elvis recorded another of Jerry's songs, the swaggering 'U.S. Male,' and romped through a very engaging version of Chuck Berry's 'Too Much Monkey Business.' The songs all had an undeniable freshness, keyed into Elvis' desire to make the best music possible with the best material available.

The next boost came from his television special, *Elvis* — widely referred to as "The Comeback Special." On June 27, 1968, he faced his first live audiences since his 1961 concert in Honolulu in two hour-long sets, encased in a tight fitting black leather suit. The shows had Elvis sitting down with his friends (including two of his original backup musicians), jamming and sharing stories. It was meant to be an informal, relaxed setting, but Elvis became increasingly nervous about it, and worried the director, Steve Binder, when he announced right before showtime he didn't think he could go on. Steve calmed him down, and got Elvis out to the stage. And as soon as he launched into the first song, 'That's All Right,' he never looked back. "He sang eight bars and he knew he had 'em," the show's music director, Bones Howe, later recalled. Two days later, on June 29, Elvis performed two more shows in his leather suit, this time standing on stage alone, and receiving another rapturous reception.

Both *Charro!* and *The Trouble With Girls* were shot after work on the Comeback Special was completed; Elvis' film commitments were fast coming to a close. The special aired in December 1968, with the first single, 'If I Can Dream,' reached #12, and the accompanying soundtrack hitting #8, Elvis' highest chart placings in three years. Fully re-energized by this new acclaim, when it was time to enter the recording studio again in January 1969 Elvis was in no mood to return to his usual routine. Instead of booking a studio in Nashville or Los Angeles, he decided to get back to where it had all began for him — in Memphis, working with producer Chips Moman

ABOVE: An 'MGM' dollar – used as a prop from the movie *The Trouble With Girls (And How To Get Into It)*, 1969.

NATIONAL BROADCASTING CO., INC.
NBC COLOR CITY
3000 W. ALAMEDA AVE., BURBANK, CALIF.

STUDIO 4
Saturday
June
29
1 9 6 8
Show Time
6:00 PM
GUESTS
SHOULD
ARRIVE
5:00 PM

"ELVIS"
starring
ELVIS PRESLEY
IN COLOR
Children Under 12 Will Not Be Admitted

LEFT: Ticket to the television show *Elvis*, later to be referred to as the 'comeback special', 1968.

BELOW: Elvis with co-star Mary Tyler Moore on the set of his last feature film, *Change Of Habit*.

at American Sound Studios.

It was one of the best decisions of Elvis' career. Hits were being made at American by a group of musicians who had such a good time in the studio they hated to leave. When informed that Elvis wanted to record at American, Chips promptly put a session with Neil Diamond on hold; he wasn't going to miss the opportunity to work with Elvis.

Two series of sessions were held at American, in January and February 1969. The musicians were immediately impressed with Elvis' work ethic, as he pushed himself through take after take on the first two nights, despite having a bad cold (which eventually caused him to bow out for a week as he was losing his voice). There was a dark tone to much of the material, alternately soulful ('Stranger In My Own Home Town'), tough ('Power Of My Love'), or bittersweet ('Gentle On My Mind'). It was the strongest material he'd been given in years, as everyone recognized as they listened to the playbacks; the musicians later recalled becoming increasingly excited at listening to songs they knew would go on to be hits. This was confirmed when "In The Ghetto," the first out of the gate, reached #3 in the charts. 'Suspicious Minds' went all the way to the top, while don't "Don't Cry Daddy" and "Kentucky Rain" reached positions 6 and 16, respectively, all singles going gold or platinum. The albums from the sessions, *From Elvis In Memphis* and *From Memphis To Vegas/From Vegas To Memphis* reached the Top Twenty and were certified gold.

Elvis had succeeded in turning his career around. There would be one final film, *Change of Habit*, which was shot after Elvis completed his work at American. Then it was time to take the next step. Elvis had got a taste of the thrill of live performance in the shows he did for the Comeback Special. Now it was time to fully reclaim the stage in live performance.

ABOVE RIGHT: Letter from Steve Binder to Colonel Parker discussing the audience ("328 young people") for Elvis' "Comeback Special", 1968.

RIGHT: Telex from Elvis to Colonel Parker, thanking him for his new MGM contract, 1966

OPPOSITE: Two images of Elvis in 1969.

STEVE BINDER

June 11, 1968

Colonel Tom Parker
Elvis Exploitations
M.G.M.
10202 West Washington Boulevard
Culver City, California 90230

Dear Colonel Parker:

It is my understanding that you will lend your help in the selection of the audience for the Elvis Presley Special. With this in mind, the following are our audience requirements:

1. 328 young people for taping of Arena segment, in their seats at 6:00 PM on saturday, June 29

2. 328 young people for second taping of Arena Segment, in their seats at 8:00 PM on saturday, June 29

I will be in touch with N.B.C. and see that they deliver to you 656 tickets for the above audience as soon as possible.

Best regards,

Steve Binder

Steve Binder

SB/gl

BINDER/HOWE PRODUCTIONS

WU TELTEX LSA

⊕

MGM INC CULV

WUC366 SSA359 L CYA204 (CT MGA455) PD

MEMPHIS TENN 27 505P CST

COLONEL TOM PARKER, MGM STUDIOS

WUX LOSA

DEAR CONONEL, ONCE AGAIN YOU HAVE PROVED YOURSELF TO BE THE
NUMBER ONE POTENTATE OF ALL TIMES. THANK YOU AGAIN FOR THE
NEW CONTRACT WITH MGM. SINCERELY

ELVIS PRESLEY

(33).

548P PST JAN 27 66

ELVIS – THE COMEBACK

On January 12, 1968, NBC announced they would be broadcasting an Elvis Christmas special that year. It was major news; Elvis hadn't appeared on TV since the Frank Sinatra special in 1960. But no one, least of all Elvis, knew the special would provide just the creative challenge he'd been looking for.

The turning point was when Steve Binder was hired to direct the special. Steve, who'd previously directed the TV music series *Hullabaloo*, wasn't that interested in Elvis or his music, but his business partner, Dayton Burr "Bones" Howe, convinced him otherwise.

Steve and Bones first met with Elvis' manager, then Elvis. Parker envisioned a traditional special, with Elvis singing holiday songs. Steve wanted to do something less conventional. Elvis agreed. The director wanted to spotlight Elvis' strengths, which Elvis was also keen to do; as the show's executive producer, Bob Finkel, wrote in in a memo to NBC and the show's sponsors, "[Elvis] wants this show to depart completely from the pattern of his motion pictures and from everything else he has done."

As work continued on the special, Priscilla noticed a change in her husband: "Each day he grew more confident and excited about his new project," she observed. The show's writers, Chris Bearde and Allan Blye, immersed themselves in Elvis' past work, and came up with an underlying theme for the show — the Jerry Reed song Elvis had recorded in 1967, 'Guitar Man.' They felt the song nicely reflected Elvis' own rags-to-riches story, and it became a key element of the show's stunning opening sequence: after a tight close up on Elvis' face as sang the opening lines of 'Trouble' (from the film *King Creole*), Elvis launched into a vibrant rendition of 'Guitar Man' as dozens of men in silhouette posed with guitars on the giant scaffolding behind him; at the end of the sequence, Elvis is standing between giant letters spelling out his name in brilliant red lights, proudly playing his

RIGHT and OPPOSITE: Two shots from the "stand up" shows taped for the special, with Elvis wearing one of his most famous outfits.

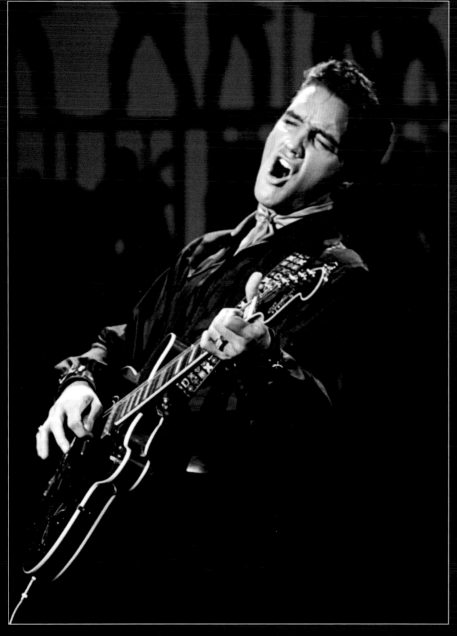

instrument, the epitome of the "swingin' little guitar man" heralded in the song.

The special's other sequences were equally impressive. There was a gospel medley, which allowed Elvis to cut loose singing his favorite music. There was an elaborate fantasy sequence, which also used 'Guitar Man' as its theme, recreating Elvis' journey from struggling singer to stardom. And when Steve noticed how Elvis like to unwind after the day's work, playing guitar and singing songs in his dressing room with his friends, it led to the show's most riveting sequences: Elvis' first live performances before an audience since 1961.

Simply titled *Elvis*, the show aired on December 3, 1968. The reviews were good and both the soundtrack album and the single 'If I Can Dream' put Elvis back in the Top 20. Elvis was fully rejuvenated — and ready to make some of the best work of his career.

LEFT: In full cry during the electrifying opening of the special.

RIGHT: Elvis' performance of "If I Can Dream" brought his TV special to an emotional close.

BELOW: Elvis during the "sit down" shows taped for the Comeback Special, when he reunited with his original guitarist, Scotty Moore, and drummer DJ Fontana.

VIVA LAS VEGAS!

The week after the Elvis Comeback Special aired, Colonel Parker began fielding numerous offers for Elvis to perform live. He decided to arrange a spectacular return to live performance for his sole client, booking a season at the International Hotel in Las Vegas. Then under construction, when finished the hotel would be the largest in Vegas: Its casino had over 1,000 slot machines; the hotel had over 1,500 rooms — at 30 stories high, it was then Nevada's tallest building; the swimming pool, with its 350,000 gallons, was the second largest body of water in the state. The Showroom Internationale, where Elvis would perform, would be able to hold up to 2,000 people.

Elvis and his manager flew to Las Vegas for a contract signing ceremony for photographers on February 26, 1969. The appearance was purely for publicity purposes; the actual contract was signed on April 15. Parker did not want Elvis to play in a brand new venue, so Barbra Streisand would be the debut performer in the showroom. Elvis was booked for a four-week engagement of two shows a night, seven nights a week, opening with a single show on July 31.

Once Elvis had completed work on his last feature film (*Change Of Habit*), he turned his thoughts to what he would like to do for his live show. He knew he wanted a full sound, and put together a rock band that would front the International's orchestra. After talking with the many musicians he knew, he decided to work with new people, and first approached guitarist James Burton. James had been in the *Louisiana Hayride* house band, and played with Rick Nelson, eventually becoming one of LA's busiest session musicians.

Elvis called James one day and the two hit it off immediately. James agreed to help Elvis put the band together, with an aim of finding musicians who had just as much passion for music as Elvis did. Elvis' sense of commitment was obvious to everyone. Bassist Jerry Scheff came to audition more out of curiosity than anything else, but was won over by how much Elvis put into his own performances, when it was the auditioning musicians who were hoping to impress. Drummer Ronnie Tutt was equally taken with Elvis. "He had such charisma, you could understand truly

why everybody was so attracted, so drawn to him," he later recalled. "I mean, the guy had it."

Rehearsals began two weeks before the July 31 opening, with the band running through over 100 numbers, Elvis clearly reveling in the opportunity to make music. Elvis didn't try to recreate his records; he wanted the music to have the kind of freshness that can only come through live performance. And he further embellished the sound by booking the Imperials, a white gospel group; the Sweet Inspirations, a black soul group; and Millie Kirkham, the soprano singer who'd appeared on a number of his records.

Elvis oversaw every aspect of the live show. He worked with designer Bill Belew in creating his outfits for the show; inspired by Elvis' interest in karate, Bill designed two-piece suits patterned after a karate *gi*, with a tunic-style top, featuring herringbone embroidery around the plunging necklines. The simple outfits were accessorized with scarves and macramé belts. And when he wasn't rehearsing, Elvis checked out other shows in Las Vegas, including Streisand's act at the International, noting how large the stage was, but assuring himself that his retinue of orchestra, band, and singers would fill it handily.

Opening night was an invitation only show, featuring a star-studded audience that included George Hamilton, Petula Clark, Cary Grant, Shirley Bassey, and Elvis' *Viva Las Vegas* co-star Ann Margret. Everyone was dazzled by a show that presented high-octane versions of Elvis' classic songs from the

ABOVE: A bill from the New Frontier hotel, Las Vegas, from 1956.

RIGHT and FAR RIGHT: Two shots from the 1969 season.

OVERLEAF: Elvis greets the press following his opening show on July 31, 1969.

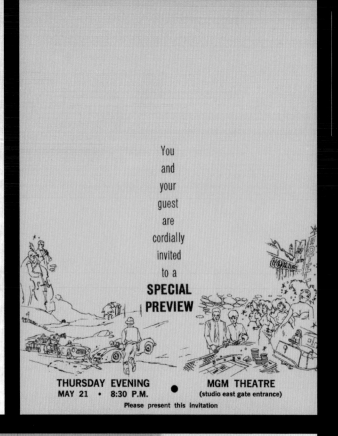

7-14-69

1. BLUE SUEDE SHOES — 2:00
2. ALL SHOOK UP — 1:50
3. ONE NIGHT — 3:00
4. LOVE ME TENDER — 3:00

Medley
1. JAILHOUSE ROCK — 1:00
2. DON'T BE CRUEL — 1:20
3. HEARTBREAK HOTEL — 2:00
4. HOUND DOG — 1:45
~~I GOT A WOMAN~~

5. MEMORIES — 3:00
6. SUCH A NIGHT — 2:10
7. MY BABE — 4:15
8. IN THE GHETTO — 3:00
9. I CAN'T STOP LOVING YOU — 3:00
10. I GOT A WOMAN — 2:30
11. JOHNNY BE GOOD — 3:25
12. THAT'S ALL RIGHT MAMA — 4:10
13. MYSTERY TRAIN AND TIGER MAN
14. WHAT'D I SAY
15.

YESTERDAY AND Hey Jude

You
and
your
guest
are
cordially
invited
to a
SPECIAL PREVIEW

THURSDAY EVENING
MAY 21 • 8:30 P.M.
●
MGM THEATRE
(studio east gate entrance)

Please present this invitation

FAR LEFT: Handwritten set list for Las Vegas rehearsals, July 14, 1969.

LEFT and BELOW: Invitation to a special preview of *Viva Las Vegas*, 1964.

METRO-GOLDWYN-MAYER
presents
ELVIS PRESLEY ANN-MARGRET
in
A JACK CUMMINGS - GEORGE SIDNEY PRODUCTION
VIVA Las VEGAS
In PANAVISION® and METROCOLOR

Co-starring CESARE DANOVA · WILLIAM DEMAREST · NICKY BLAIR · Written by SALLY BENSON · Directed by GEORGE SIDNEY

1950s ('That's All Right,' 'Heartbreak Hotel,' 'All Shook Up'), contemporary material ('I Can't Stop Loving You'), and his recent hits ('In The Ghetto,' 'Suspicious Minds'). Elvis received a standing ovation when he first walked on stage, before he had even sung a single note. "I could see the look change on his face," Jerry Scheff recalled. "It's like, 'Oh God, they still love me!'" And they did. Elvis' four-week run was completely sold out, and the success of 'Suspicious Minds,' released at the end of August was the icing on the cake. The single adopted the ending Elvis gave it in the show, with an extended coda that fades out then fades back up. The single shot straight to #1 and became another million seller. A live album of the engagement was also released, first as part of the *From Memphis To Vegas/From Vegas To Memphis* double album set, then as the stand-alone album *Elvis In Person At The International Hotel*. In comparison to his first run of Vegas shows back in 1956, it was indeed a triumphant return.

Plans for a return engagement were firmed up before the 1969 season had closed. Elvis returned to the International in January 1970, with a four week run from January 26 to February 23. There were various changes to the show. The 1969 shows had relied heavily on songs from Elvis' catalogue; the 1970 shows drew on more contemporary material, including Creedence Clearwater Revival's 'Proud Mary,' Joe South's 'Walk A Mile In My Shoes,' and Neil Diamond's 'Sweet Caroline.' Tony Joe White's 'Polk Salad Annie' became a showstopper to rival 'Suspicious Minds,' complete with karate moves. It was during this engagement that Elvis began wearing jumpsuits, the costume that would become

his trademark. With the jumpsuits, he had greater freedom of movement, especially when he did one of his high karate kicks. During 'Love Me Tender' he would sometimes make his way around the showroom, bestowing kisses on lucky fans. There was another live album drawn from the run, *On Stage*; the accompanying single, a live version of 'The Wonder Of You,' hit the Top 10 in the US and topped the charts in the UK.

Elvis' Vegas routine was now set. Through the end of 1976, he would generally do two Vegas stints a year, in the winter and summer, when the engagement was known as the "Elvis Summer Festival." Fans regularly traveled from all over the world selling out the showroom and the hotel (which became the Las Vegas Hilton in 1971). Elvis had always loved experiencing the nightlife in the city that never slept; now he was one of Las Vegas' top attractions.

With his first two Vegas seasons documented by live albums, something special was planned for his third Vegas engagement, which ran from August 10 to September 7; a documentary film would be made. *Elvis: That's The Way It Is* captured rehearsals in LA and Las Vegas, along with plenty of live concert footage. It remains the best record of Elvis in his '70s prime. And there were dramatic new additions to the set list, with 'You've Lost That Loving Feeling' and 'Bridge Over Troubled Water.'

Elvis: That's The Way It Is was released in November 1970; now, people who wondered what Elvis' Las Vegas show was like could see for themselves. But soon enough they wouldn't have to go all the way to Las Vegas to see him. Elvis was getting his act together and taking it the road.

E. A. PRESLEY
3764 HIGHWAY 51. SOUTH
MEMPHIS, TENNESSEE

3254

July 17 19 70

PAY TO THE ORDER OF ___ CASH ___ $ 500 00

Five Hundred Dollars

DOLLARS

E. A. PRESLEY

NBC National Bank of Commerce
Memphis, Tennessee

Personal cash for Elvis in Las Vegas.

OPPOSITE AND PREVIOUS PAGE: During his 1969 season, Elvis alternated between simple two-piece outfits in black, navy, or white. The 1969 shows featured much of his older material; later shows had more contemporary hits.

LEFT: Check to "cash" for Elvis in Las Vegas, 1970.

FROM ELVIS IN MEMPHIS

The sessions at American Sound Studios in early 1969 had resulted in an embarrassment of riches for Elvis; a total of 31 songs to draw on for his next album. Twelve were ultimately selected for From Elvis In Memphis. *The front cover had a supremely confident looking Elvis from the opening sequence of his recent television special. And the music inside evinced a new maturity; songs that acknowledged life's struggles as well as its joys.*

Released: June 1969
Chart position: #13

From Elvis In Memphis is an album very much steeped in soul; even the country numbers have a touch of the blues. The album begins with a solemn organ chord, and an extended, slow opening, until the drums kick in, the song hits its groove, and Elvis lightheartedly bemoans the antics of his faithless girlfriend in 'Wearin' That Loved On Look.' 'Only The Strong Survive,' with its spoken word intro about a mother passing on advice to her son, might have been written with Elvis in mind, and he strikes just the right note of heartfelt sympathy.

Elvis plays the piano himself on Eddy Arnold's 'I'll Hold You In My Heart (Till I Can Hold You In My Arms),' conjuring up a feeling of late night ambience, the last song played for the night before the musicians head for home. Next up, the stark 'Long Black Limousine' features one of Elvis' most passionate vocals as he sings of losing his love twice; once when she heads off to the city in search of fame and fortune, and a second time when she returns in a hearse. 'It Keeps Right On A-Hurtin'' is another song of regret, delivered with a delicate sensitivity.

The songs may deal with problematic relationships, but not every number is downbeat. 'I'm Movin' On' had been a hit for Hank Snow, and was also about the end of a relationship, but here the mood is celebratory — it's Elvis doing the leaving! 'Power Of My Love' has a similar swaggering boldness, with a tough, aggressive vocal from Elvis, emphasized by phrases like "push it, pound it."

Then it was back to lost love with 'Gentle On My Mind,' previously a big hit for Glen Campbell. In contrast to Campbell's more upbeat version, Elvis chose to slow down the tempo and injects a strong sense of poignancy into his vocal; the final image of the singer drinking soup in a train yard while wishing the cup he's holding is his lover is particularly haunting.

Elvis knew 'After Loving You' from Eddy Arnold and Della Reese's versions, and he throws himself into the song, delivering a rich, full-bodied vocal. 'True Love Travels On A Gravel Road' looks at relationships from a unique angle, pointing out that difficulties can actually bring a couple closer together, a point Elvis drives home with empathy. And he sounds suitably anxious on 'Any Day Now,' a depiction of a relationship on the verge of crumbling, as he sorrowfully notes, "Any day now/ love will let me down."

The album concludes with 'In The Ghetto,' another song that told a clear story, the tale of a boy raised in deprivation who grows up to meet a tragic fate. Elvis rarely made overt "statements" in his songs, frequently insisting he was just an entertainer. But the compelling drama of the number touched a nerve, and he gave the song one of the finest vocal performances of his career.

Elvis had opened the decade in classic style with *Elvis Is Back!* Now he saw the decade out with another classic piece of work. From start to finish, *From Elvis In Memphis* is a grand accomplishment.

OPPOSITE: Elvis with the "Memphis Boys" – the house band at American Sound Studio: Bobby Wood, Mike Leech, Tommy Cogbill, Gene Chrisman, Elvis, Bobby Emmons, Reggie Young, Ed Kollis and Dan Penn. The photograph was taken in January 1969.

ON THE ROAD AGAIN

Elvis spent most of his career in the 1970s on tour. He first performed outside of Las Vegas in a run of five concerts at the Texas Livestock Show, held at the Houston Astrodome, February 27 to March 1, 1970, including an evening show on February 28 which drew a record-breaking 43,000 people. That fall, he went out on short tours during September and November, and spent the next seven years crisscrossing the country, performing to the adoring crowds that were always there to meet him.

One of the most remarkable events of Elvis' life happened in December 1970 when he met President Richard Nixon. Elvis had unexpectedly left his home in Memphis and ended up in Los Angeles, where he contacted his friend, Jerry Schilling, and arranged for the two of them to fly to Washington, D.C.. He dropped off a handwritten letter to President Nixon to a startled guard at the White House gates, and was later summoned to the White House by Nixon aide Egil "Bud" Krogh, who happened to be an Elvis fan and thought these two strong personalities should get together. "I was just enthralled with the idea of these two guys meeting each other," Bud explained. Elvis offered his services to the country, and was rewarded with his very own badge from the Bureau of Narcotics and Dangerous Drugs. The President wrote Elvis a letter at the end of the year, writing "It was a pleasure to meet with you in my office recently," and wishing Elvis and his family all the best for the coming year.

1971 began with Elvis honored by the Junior Chamber of Commerce in America as one of the country's "Ten Outstanding Young Men Of The Year." Elvis proudly hosted a cocktail reception for all the winners and their guests at Graceland on January 16, prior to the awards ceremony that evening at the Ellis Auditorium. And his pride was also evident in the speech he delivered when he was given his award. "When I was a child, ladies and gentlemen, I was a dreamer. I read comic books, and I was the hero of the comic book. I saw movies, and I was the hero in the movie. So every dream that I ever dreamed has come through a hundred times." And he reaffirmed his faith in what had brought him to this peak when he closed his speech by observing: "I'd like to say that I learned

very early in life that 'Without a song day would never end, without a song a man ain't got a friend, without a song the road would never bend, without a song' — so I keep singing a song."

And there were more career milestones ahead. On August 28, 1971, Elvis received the Bing Crosby Award — now known as the Lifetime Achievement award — from the National Academy of Recording Arts and Sciences, the organization that puts on the annual Grammy Awards. Elvis would go on to win two more Grammy awards in the 1970s, for "Best Inspirational Performance" for his 1972 album *He Touched Me*, and for the version of 'How Great Thou Art' that appeared on the 1974 album *Elvis Recorded Live On Stage In Memphis*.

Elvis' first-ever concerts in New York City, held in June 1972, drew record crowds, making Elvis the first performer to sell out four consecutive shows at the venue. Elvis' second documentary film, *Elvis On Tour*, filmed and released in 1972, went on to win the Golden Globe for best documentary. His landmark *Aloha From Hawaii* show, a live satellite broadcast held on January 14, 1973, was the first of its kind, drawing a record viewing audience, bringing in over $75,000 in charity donations (for the Kui Lee Cancer Fund), and producing another live album, this one topping the charts.

There were more musical accomplishments too. *Elvis Country*, released in 1970 brought Elvis back to his roots, while his second holiday album, *Elvis Sings The Wonderful World Of Christmas*, released in 1971, became as much of a steady seller as his first Christmas release. 'Burning Love,' released in 1972, went all the way to #2 and gave him another million seller.

OPPOSITE: Rehearsing for his upcoming Las Vegas dates in the summer of 1970. Rehearsals, and the shows, were filmed for the documentary *Elvis: That's The Way It Is.*

LEFT and RIGHT: Two further images from the rehearsals and shows filmed for the documentary *Elvis: That's The Way It Is.*

BELOW: Elvis poses for the pictures needed for the honorary police badge he received from the Denver Police Department in 1970. Elvis met many police officers on the road when he returned to touring, and always looked forward to adding a new badge to his collection.

'Separate Ways,' which came out in 1972 and was a Top 20 hit, also unexpectedly reflected Elvis' personal life. 1972 was the year he and Priscilla separated, with the divorce becoming final in 1973. Elvis' return to the road had taken a toll on his marriage, and, increasingly, his health. His new girlfriend, Linda Thompson, helped keep his spirits up. "I was very happy to share life with him," she said.

Elvis now began to spend more time working in Memphis. He recorded at Stax Studios in July and December 1973 — the first Memphis sessions since 1969 — using musicians from his current live band, as well as those he'd recorded with in Memphis in 1969 and Nashville in the early 1970s. His songs now began hitting the country charts; albums with tracks from these sessions, *Good Times* and *Promised Land*, reached the Top 10 in the country charts, as did the singles 'I've Got A Thing About You Baby' and 'Promised Land.' Back in 1954, when Elvis met Ernest Tubb, he told the country star that while he was making money with rock 'n' roll, what he really wanted to do was to sing country. Ernest advised him "Do what they tell you to do. Make your money. Then you can do what *you* want to do." Elvis had done so — and now he was back singing the country music he'd always loved.

In 1974, Elvis gave his first concerts in Memphis since 1961, at the Mid-South Coliseum, and *Elvis Recorded Live On Stage In Memphis* gave Elvis another Top 40 hit. In January and February 1976, and October 1976, recording sessions were held at Graceland, with the studio set up in Graceland's den — the "Jungle Room." Songs recorded during these sessions appeared on the albums *From Elvis Presley Boulevard, Memphis, Tennessee* (1976) and *Moody Blue* (1977), both of which topped the country charts. Singles from the sessions performed just as well, with 'Hurt,' 'Moody Blue,' and 'Way Down' all hitting the Top 10. Elvis' first national hits had been on the country charts, some 20 years later, that's where he still had a home.

1977 was filled with the usual slate of tours: short jaunts in mid-February; early March; mid-April to early May; mid-May to early June; and mid-June to the end of the month. There were cameras in the audience for two shows, shooting for a planned TV special. The final night of the tour was June 26 in Indianapolis, Indiana, Colonel Parker's 68th birthday. Over the

course of an 80-minute concert, Elvis, wearing a jumpsuit emblazoned with a golden Aztec-inspired sundial, performed his early hits ('Hound Dog,' 'Jailhouse Rock'), a little country ('I Really Don't Want To Know'), a little R&B ('What'd I Say'), and, as usual, wowed the crowd with stirring renditions of 'Bridge Over Troubled Water' and 'Hurt.'

It was Elvis' last live show.

ABOVE and RIGHT: Elvis playing one of his favorite guitars, a Gibson J-200, during rehearsals for his 1970 Vegas summer season.

STANDING ROOM ONLY: THE CONCERT FILMS

Change of Habit was the last feature film Elvis made, but it wasn't his last movie. Two concert films were released during the 1970s, Elvis: That's The Way It Is *and* Elvis On Tour.

The success of Elvis' return to live performance in Las Vegas made a documentary about one of his Vegas engagements a logical choice. So when Elvis began rehearsing for his dates at the International Hotel during August and September 1970, film cameras were there from the very beginning. Elvis and the musicians are seen rehearsing and fooling around with an easy camaraderie. He's shown as someone always ready to crack a joke, but nonetheless clearly in charge, patiently going over a song's ending until he gets it right. Even if a number has been

LEFT and RIGHT: Elvis in 1972; several shows on his tour were filmed that year and featured in the documentary *Elvis On Tour.*

performed before, Elvis attacks it like it's a new addition to the set list. Rehearsals are a lot of fun, but also clearly a lot of work.

An interesting aspect of the film are the sequences that don't involve Elvis; the fans who talk about their devotion to their idol, the hotel staff shown attending to every aspect of the engagement. On opening night, Elvis is seen nonchalantly reading congratulatory telegrams ("Here's hoping that you have a very successful opening and that you break both legs. Tom Jones"), but his nervousness is clear to see.

The last hour of the film is devoted to the live show. The songs are primarily recent numbers, with Elvis building up to suitably dramatic endings for 'You've Lost That Loving Feeling' and 'Bridge Over Troubled Water,' while 'Polk Salad Annie' shows how some songs are best experienced live in concert, and not just on record. But the showstopper is undoubtedly 'Suspicious Minds,' an energetic version that brings down the house; it's worth seeing the film for this performance alone. The film was released in November 1970. In 2001, a newly edited "Special Edition" of the film was released on DVD; a later 2007 edition featured both the original 1970 theatrical release and the 2001 cut.

Elvis On Tour was a road film, with performances drawn from a number of shows on Elvis' April 1972 tour. While there are some rehearsal scenes, most of the footage features live material. There's a clear sense of how isolating life on the road could be, showing Elvis going from plane to limo, limo to backstage, backstage to the performance, then taking the same route in reverse after the show. While onstage, he's a figure of palpable energy; offstage, as people bustle around him, he's the eye of calm in the center of the storm.

There's a bit of backstory in the middle of film. How did Elvis get to where he is? Clips from his first Ed Sullivan appearance show a fresh-faced, bright-eyed youngster who's eager to please, contrasting with the assured confidence of the latter-day Elvis. Another nice moment comes when Elvis is seen singing gospel numbers with J.D. Sumner and the Stamps quartet; losing himself, as always, in the music he loved to sing.

Elvis' desire to please his audience is seen as being just as strong as it was in the 1950s. 'Love

Me Tender' becomes a fun free-for-all as women rush to the stage to get a kiss. The emotional high point is the patriotic medley 'An American Trilogy,' though 'You Gave Me A Mountain' runs a close second. Even the dizzying array of jumpsuits adds to the excitement. *Elvis On Tour*, which opened in November 1972, also added to Elvis' array of honors, winning the Golden Globe for Best Documentary.

BELOW: Hand-amended credit list for *That's The Way It Is* with Elvis' personal notes in blue ink and Colonel Tom Parker's notes in black.

RIGHT: Poster from Elvis: *That's The Way It Is*, 1970.

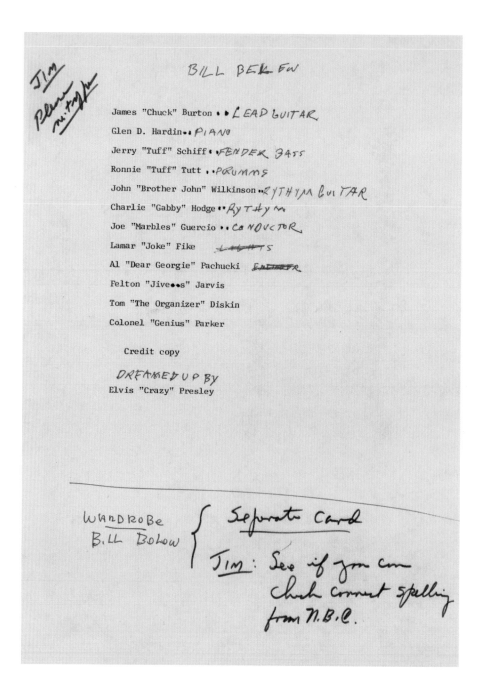

a film about him

ELVIS

"that's the way it is."

SEE ELVIS SING The Next Step Is Love • Polk Salad Annie • Stranger in the Crowd • Love Me Tender Bridge Over Troubled Waters • You've Lost That Lovin' Feelin' • Blue Suede Shoes Heartbreak Hotel • You Don't Have To Say You Love Me • All Shook Up • Patch It Up Can't Help Falling In Love With You • Suspicious Minds • I Just Can't Help Believing —and many others!

Metro-Goldwyn-Mayer presents ELVIS PRESLEY in **"THAT'S THE WAY IT IS"** directed by DENIS SANDERS • PANAVISION® • METROCOLOR

ROCK MY SOUL

"I know practically every religious song that's ever been written," Elvis once told a reporter. It was no idle boast. Elvis grew up singing the songs he heard in church, and gospel tunes and hymns were among the first songs he learned to play on guitar. He loved to warm up before recording sessions and unwind after concerts by singing religious songs.

So it was no surprise that after he became a recording artist, he released a record of religious music as soon as he could. On January 6, 1957, he sang 'Peace in the Valley' on *The Ed Sullivan Show*, and six days later he was in the studio recording the song for the EP of the same name. The song was written by Thomas A. Dorsey, and Elvis recorded another song by Dorsey for the EP, 'Take My Hand, Precious Lord,' as well as 'It Is No Secret (What God Can Do)' and 'I Believe,' an inspirational song recorded by one of Elvis' favorite singers, Roy Hamilton. In addition to appearing on the *Peace In The Valley* EP, the four songs were also placed on *Elvis' Christmas Album*, also released in 1957.

The EP had sold over 400,000 copies, sales strong enough to spark interest in future religious recordings by Elvis, so in 1960 he entered the studio to record his first religious album, *His Hand In Mine*. Elvis drew on a number of songs from his favorite gospel groups, the Blackwood Brothers and the Statesmen, for the album, including the Blackwood's 'Mansion Over the Hilltop' and 'In My Father's House,' and the Statesmen's 'His Hand In Mine,' 'I Believe In The Man In The Sky,' and 'He Knows Just What I Need'; 'Known Only To Him' was a song recorded by both groups.

Elvis' sublime performances of those songs had the kind of reverence traditionally associated with religious numbers. But he recorded livelier numbers for the album as well. His friend Charlie Hodge had introduced Elvis to the work of the Golden Gate Quartet, who'd recorded 'Swing Down Sweet Chariot' and 'Joshua Fit The Battle,' songs Elvis performs here in rousing fashion. The black gospel numbers 'Milky White Way' and 'Working On The

Building' have a similar engaging energy and a bluesy swing. Even Elvis' backing singers, the Jorndanaires, provided a song, 'I'm Gonna Walk Dem Golden Stairs,' written by a former member of the group, Cully Holt. The album reached #13 in the charts, and sold over a million copies — impressive for a pop album, and excellent for a religious one.

One song recorded at the session, 'Crying in the Chapel,' wasn't included on the album. When it was released as a single five years later, it became a big hit, going to #3 in the US, topping the charts in the UK: it sold over a million copies, bringing the idea of making another religious album to the forefront. Elvis was excited about making another religious recording and arranged to have the Imperials, a gospel group founded by former Statesmen Jake Hess, at the sessions. Along with the Jordanaires, three female backing vocalists, and Elvis, there were 12 voices on the album, providing a rich, full sound. "Elvis just really loved that sound; the adrenaline really pumped in him when he heard it," Jake Hess recalled. "He just wanted that big sound."

He returned to the Statesmen's songbook with the gentle 'Without Him,' and 'Where No One Stands Alone,' the latter number featuring an especially impressive vocal performance by Elvis. The finger snaps give 'Where Could I Go But To The Lord' an undeniably "cool" edge, making the song as much a blues as it was a gospel number. And the uptempo numbers never fail to raise the spirits, as 'If The Lord Wasn't Walking By My Side,' by the Imperials' piano player, Henry Slaughter, does so handily. 'By And By,' and the Golden Gate Quartet's 'Run On' are equally invigorating. Elvis also drew on songs by the Harmonizing Four; Elvis greatly admired the group's singer, Jimmy Jones, and had tried to book him

ABOVE: *He Touched Me*, released in 1972, won the Grammy for Best Inspirational Performance; *His Hand In Mine*, released in 1960, was Elvis' first album of sacred music.

RIGHT: Elvis singing with the Jordanaires backing him up.

for the sessions, but Jones couldn't be located. 'So High' has a bright bounce, while 'Farther Along' and 'Somebody Bigger Than You And I' are all moving and sincere performances.

It was 'How Great Thou Art,' another song previously done by the Statesmen, that would be the standout track of the session and would become the album's title track. Elvis' stirring rendition builds to a dramatic climax in the song's final notes. To Jerry Schilling, who watched Elvis record the song, it was clear his friend poured his heart and soul into the performance, leaving him drained: "It was as if something happened outside the normal experience,"

Jerry recalled. How fitting then that *How Great Thou Art*, released in 1967, won Elvis' first Grammy, receiving the award for "Best Sacred Performance." The album was a Top 20 hit, eventually selling over two million copies.

In 1971, a number of Elvis' previously recorded inspirational songs were brought together on the album *You'll Never Walk Alone*, including as 'Let Us Pray' (from *Change Of Habit*) and the title track, a song from the musical *Carousel* that had previously been recorded by Roy Hamilton. That same year, it was decided the time was right for a new religious album. The Imperials again provided backing vocals,

ABOVE LEFT: Elvis' Grammy awards were all for his religious recordings.

ABOVE: Elvis loved to warm up for a recording session by singing hymns and gospel songs.

Elvis Presley

and it was the group's signature song, 'He Touched Me,' that would give the album its title.

This record would have a more modern feel and sound than the previously religious albums — this can be heard in 'I've Got Confidence,' originally by black gospel artist Andrae Crouch. 'Seeing Is Believing' was co-written by Elvis' friend Red West and keyboard player/arranger Glen Spreen, while 'A Thing Called Love' was another by Jerry "Guitar Man" Reed. But there was older, more traditional material as well, such as 'An Evening Prayer,' which Elvis knew from gospel singer Mahalia Jackson's version. 'Bosom Of Abraham' and 'I, John' were a return to the uptempo spirits of 'Run On' and 'So High.' There was also a slow, bluesy version of one of the world's best known hymns, 'Amazing Grace.' *He Touched Me*, released in in 1972, would go on to win a Grammy for "Best Inspirational Performance."

He Touched Me was Elvis' last religious album, but he would continue to record and perform inspirational music, both in the studio and in his concerts. It was a live rendition of 'How Great Thou Art' that appeared on the 1974 album *Elvis As Recorded Live On Stage In Memphis* that would bring Elvis his next Grammy, when the song won the "Best Inspirational Performance" award. It was a song that had become a showstopper in Elvis' live act.

Religious music also provided much solace to Elvis over the years, one reason why he so loved singing hymns with his friends. Ultimately, it was the music that was closest to his heart. The last album that Elvis listened to on the record player in his bedroom was a new release by one of his favorite gospel acts, J.D. Sumner and The Stamps, who had previously sung with him in concert.

RIGHT: Elvis seen in the suit he wore on the cover of *His Hand In Mine*.

DOWN HOME COUNTRY BOY

Most people think of Elvis as a rock 'n' roller, but he has strong ties to country music too. Both his first and his last hits were on the country charts. His first record featured a country song, and he made his debut radio performance on one of the top-rated country shows of its day. And the first song he sang in public was a country song; Elvis won his first prize when he sang Red Foley's 'Old Shep' at the Mississippi-Alabama Fair and Dairy Show in Tupelo in 1945.

Nine years later, when looking for a B-side for his first single, it was Elvis' bassist Bill Black who began playing Bill Monroe's 'Blue Moon Of Kentucky' in the studio, leading to its becoming the flip side of 'That's All Right.' Its appeal was soon obvious; the month after the single's release, the song was at #3 on *Billboard*'s Country & Western Territorial Best Sellers chart (which tracked sales in different regions around the United States).

Producer Sam Phillips parlayed this into landing Elvis an appearance on the Grand Ole Opry on October 2, 1954. The Opry was (and remains) a weekly country show held in Nashville every Saturday night and broadcast on the radio, and Elvis performed 'Blue Moon Of Kentucky' during the segment of the show hosted by Hank Snow. Elvis also met Bill Monroe that night, disarming the older singer by saying how much he and his mother liked Monroe's songs. Monroe informed Elvis that not only did he enjoy Elvis' version of his song, he'd re-recorded the song himself, opening in the original tempo, then following Elvis' lead and going into 4/4 time.

Elvis was then booked to appear on another country show, the *Louisiana Hayride*, broadcast every Saturday night from Shreveport, Louisiana; artists like Hank Williams, Kitty Wells, and Jim Reeves had all got their start on the program. After his debut on October 16, 1954, Elvis landed a regular spot on the show, which helped to boost his profile. By the end of 1954, he was named 8th Most Promising Country & Western Artist in *Billboard*'s annual disc jockey poll.

For the next few years, Elvis toured with a variety of country acts, including Hank Snow, Mother Maybelle and the Carter Sisters, Faron Young,

George Jones, and the Duke of Paducah. When he first met singer Wanda Jackson on such a tour, she initially thought he was "just another country singer." That changed when she saw him perform — and heard how his reworking of country songs put new life into the genre. "He was fresh, and new, and young, energetic, and it was a whole new era being born," she said. "No one had ever seen anything like him. I don't think they've seen many like him since, that just absolutely changed the whole music industry. Just turned it upside down. These big pop singers that had big hits in the pop field, all of a sudden this kid comes along that's taking record sales away from them. He just singlehandedly turned our business upside down."

By the time he signed with RCA, Elvis' singles had moved from the regional to the national country charts: 'Baby Let's Play House' reached #5, while both sides of Elvis' last Sun single, "I Forgot To Remember To Forget'/'Mystery Train' hit the country chart, the latter peaking at #10, the former going all the way to #1. Yet when he moved onto the pop charts, the country hits still remained: 'Heartbreak Hotel' was #1 on both pop and country; 'I Want You, I Need You, I Love You' was #3 pop, #1 country; and 'Don't Be Cruel'/ 'Hound Dog' not only topped the pop and country charts, it topped the R&B charts as well. Country songs continued to appear on his albums as well: 'When My Blue Moon Turns To Gold Again' (on *Elvis*); 'A Fool Such As I,' a hit for Hank Snow which reached #2 in Elvis' version; and, fittingly, 'Old Shep,' which found a place on the *Elvis* album.

Elvis' first films also highlighted his country background. *Love Me Tender* had a rural setting, and featured the country-flavored songs 'We're Gonna

ABOVE: Welcome to *Elvis Country* — the name of Elvis 1970 studio album, recorded in Nashville.

RIGHT: Elvis as seen in the film *Flaming Star*.

Move,' 'Poor Boy' and 'Let Me' — though his dance moves were a bit anachronistic for the Civil War era in which the film was set. *Loving You* also played up Elvis' country roots, with the song 'Lonesome Cowboy' driving the point home.

For the first part of the 1960s, Elvis' musical style became more cosmopolitan — as a hit like 'It's Now Or Never' can attest — but country was never very far away. Elvis' version of Hank Williams' 'Your Cheatin' Heart,' originally recorded in 1958, was finally released on the 1965 album *Elvis For Everyone*. The same 1967 session where Elvis jumped on the country-

rock bandwagon with Jerry Reed's 'Guitar Man' also saw him record the country standard 'Just Call Me Lonesome.' And he revisited a number of country numbers during his landmark sessions at American Sound Studios in 1969 — 'Gentle On My Mind,' 'From A Jack To A King,' 'I'll Hold You In My Heart,' 'It Keeps Right On A-Hurtin'' — while creating a new country classic of his own with 'Kentucky Rain.'

The album with the strongest country theme was of course *Elvis Country*, released in January 1971, with the gospel standard 'I Was Born About Ten Thousand Years Ago' linking the album's 12 tracks together. The

ABOVE: Elvis frequently adopted a cowboy look for his films: as the son of a Native American woman and white man in *Flaming Star*.

RIGHT: Elvis as a full-blooded Native American in *Stay Away, Joe*.

album encompassed a diverse range of country styles, from the classics (Bill Monroe's 'Little Cabin On The Hill,' Eddy Arnold's 'I Really Don't Want To Know' and 'Make the World Go Away,' Bob Wills' 'Faded Love,' Ernest Tubb's 'Tomorrow Never Comes') to more modern examples of the genre (Anne Murray's 'Snowbird,' Willie Nelson's 'Funny How Time Slips Away'). As always, Elvis stamped his own personality on the material — just listen to the fantastically lively covers of Jerry Lee Lewis' 'Whole Lotta Shakin' Goin' On' and the equally vibrant 'I Washed My Hands In Muddy Water,' a number previously recorded by Charlie Rich, Johnny Rivers, and Stonewall Jackson. Another highlight is his funky reworking of Sanford Clark's 'The Fool.' The album reached the Top 20 on both the pop and country charts.

In the latter part of his career, Elvis' records were most successful on the country charts. From 1974 to 1977 he had eight Top 20 country singles, and ten Top 10 country albums (*Promised Land* and *From Elvis Presley Boulevard, Memphis, Tennessee* going to #1). And the last #1 records Elvis had during his lifetime were on the country charts, when both the 'Moody Blue' single, and the album of the same name topped their respective charts.

Country music remained close to Elvis' heart until the very end. The last song he recorded, in October 1976 in the den at Graceland, was Jim Reeves' 'He'll Have To Go.' Ten months later, in the early morning hours of August 16, 1977, Elvis, his girlfriend Ginger Alden, and his cousin Billy Smith and his wife Jo went to the racquetball building on Graceland's grounds for a quick game. Afterwards, Elvis sat at the piano and played a few songs for the group. The last number he played for his friends was Willie Nelson's 'Blue Eyes Crying In The Rain.'

BELOW LEFT: Western splendor as the aspiring singer in *Loving You*.

BELOW RIGHT: A portrait from *King Creole*.

RIGHT: In Elvis' first film, *Love Me Tender*, he gave a country swing to songs like the folk song 'We're Gonna Move.'

ELVIS ON 45

For much of his career, Elvis' chart hits didn't appear on his albums. Indeed, many of his most famous songs were initially released only on singles — and on some occasions the B-side would chart nearly as high as the main side.

Elvis' records on the Sun label were all singles-only releases. And his national breakthrough came with his first RCA single, 'Heartbreak Hotel.' The stark, almost brooding number had a much darker feel than the freewheeling spirit evident on the Sun releases, but it was Elvis' first bonafide smash, topping the charts and selling a million copies in just three months. The yearning ballad 'I Want You, I Need You, I Love You' displayed yet another side of rock 'n' roll's newest star. But it was Elvis' next single, 'Don't Be Cruel'/'Hound Dog,' that delivered the knockout punch in that breakout year. 'Don't Be Cruel' was a swinging piece of pop, while 'Hound Dog' roared out of the starting gate with a ferocious energy and a particularly stinging guitar line by Scotty Moore. The single became a double-sided hit for Elvis, with both sides not only sharing the #1 position on the pop charts, but topping the Country and R&B charts as well.

No soundtrack albums were released for *Love Me Tender* or *Jailhouse Rock*; the title songs initially only appeared on singles (and EPs). 'Love Me Tender' is the kind of ballad one can imagine Elvis singing in the pre-Sun days; 'Jailhouse Rock' was a lyrically clever number about prisoners so happy rocking out they couldn't care less about breaking out. Both songs topped the charts. The rollicking 'Too Much' was yet another #1, as was the breezy pop of 'All Shook Up,' and the simmering 'Don't.' The importance of songs like 'Wear My Ring Around Your Neck,' 'One Night,' 'A Fool Such As I,' and 'A Big Hunk O' Love' wasn't just that they all reached the Top 5; it's also because they were released during the years when Elvis was in the army, and helped keep his profile high.

Elvis' first post-army single, 'Stuck On You,' put him back on top with a song that echoed the lighthearted feel of 'Don't Be Cruel' and 'All Shook Up.' But his next non-album singles revealed a dramatically different Elvis. Both 'It's Now Or Never' and 'Surrender' were bold Neapolitan-flavored numbers (the melody of the former dating back to 1898), that required an operatic reach from Elvis — especially on the thrilling high notes that conclude both songs. 'Are You Lonesome Tonight?' was a tender ballad with a spoken word section that tugged on the heartstrings, and that would return to Elvis' live repertoire for his final tour.

'His Latest Flame'/'Little Sister' was another double-sided hit, two irresistible pop songs that each crashed into the Top 5. 'Good Luck Charm' and 'Devil In Disguise' continued the tradition of strong non-album singles, both topping the charts.

Another great run of non-album singles resulted from the American Sound Studios sessions in January-February 1969. 'Suspicious Minds' was one of Elvis' biggest hits, selling well over a million copies and a centerpiece of his live show. The theme of trying to repair broken relationships was also present in the more contemplative 'Don't Cry Daddy' and the underlying determination of 'Kentucky Rain,' all songs of deep, heartfelt emotion.

And on occasion, a single had its greatest success in another country. A version of the patriotic medley 'An American Trilogy' from Elvis' February 1972 season in Las Vegas charted low in the US but soared into the Top 10 in the UK, a nation whose Elvis fans are known for their exceptional devotion.

OPPOSITE and OVERLEAF:
A selection of single releases that did not initially appear on albums.

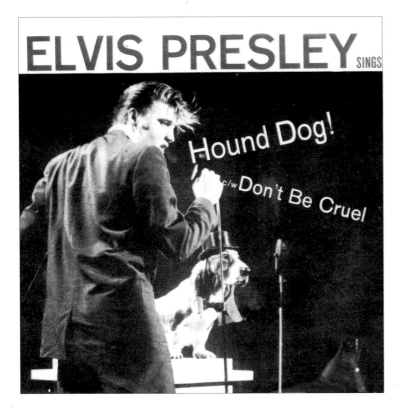

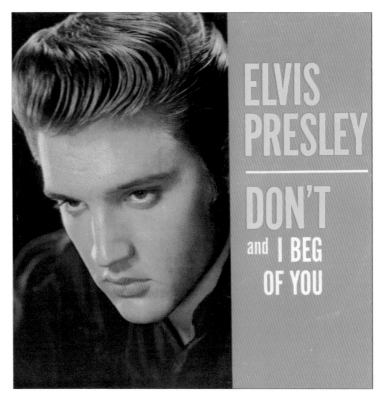

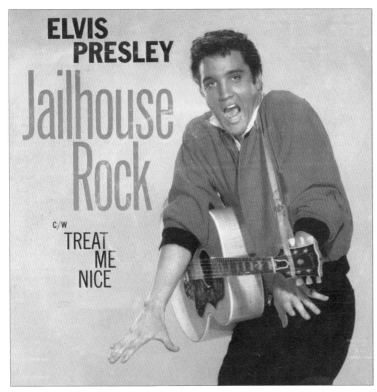

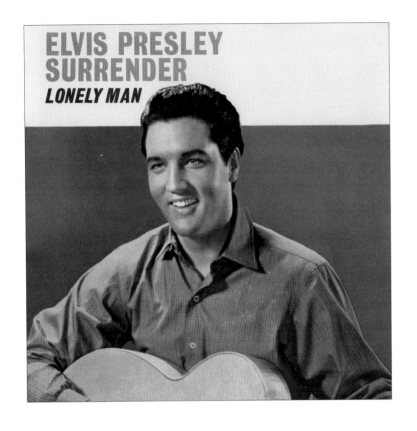

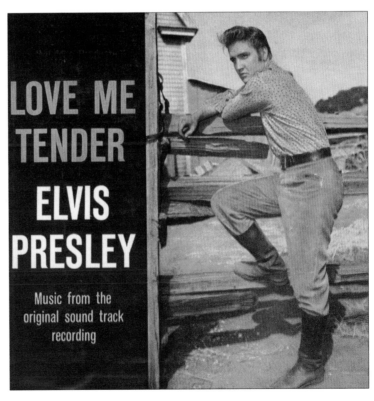

STATE OF GRACE(LAND)

In March 1957, Elvis bought Graceland, which would be his Memphis home for the next 20 years. Graceland is located eight miles south of downtown Memphis, in the city's Whitehaven neighborhood. The Graceland mansion, and the 13 acres that surround it, were originally part of a 500-acre property called Graceland Farms; the original owner, S.E. Toof, named the farm after his daughter, Grace. In 1939, Grace's niece Ruth Moore and her husband Dr. Thomas Moore built the mansion, which also took on the name Graceland.

As Elvis' career took off, he had moved into increasingly larger residences; from 1954 to 1957, Elvis and his parents lived in four different homes. The last was a three-bedroom ranch-style house on Audubon Drive, in a suburban neighborhood east of downtown. It was the nicest place the family had ever lived, but due to the continual parade of fans who came through the neighborhood hoping to get a glimpse of the young star, Elvis decided that he needed a place with greater privacy.

In March 1957, Elvis was completing work on the film *Loving You* in California, when he received a call from his parents saying they'd found just such a place. He returned to Memphis on March 18, went out to see Graceland the following day, and decided to buy it, putting down $1,000 as a deposit. The deal was finalized on March 25, with a final price of $102,500. Registration of the purchase was filed on March 28, 1957 and recorded the next day. Graceland was his.

Elvis made a lot of renovations to his new home, proudly telling a reporter "This is going to be a lot nicer than Red Skelton's house when I get it like I want it." He constructed a wall along the front, made of Alabama fieldstone. He also commissioned a special set of wrought iron gates for the main entrance, decorated with a music staff, music notes, and his own silhouette.

Among the buildings on the property were a barn an office, a smokehouse, and the two-story Georgian colonial style mansion itself, which had a suitably grand entryway with four Corinthian columns flanking the front portico, and a facade of Mississippi fieldstone. Elvis soon added a swimming pool and built a two-tiered patio beside it. He outfitted his

master bedroom, on the second floor with a massive nine-foot square bed — when you stand outside the mansion, facing the front door, the two windows on the upper right are where Elvis' bedroom was). His grandmother, Minnie Mae Presley, lived in another bedroom on the second floor; it would later be Lisa Marie's room. Elvis' parents stayed in a bedroom downstairs; when Vernon remarried, he moved into a house around the corner from Graceland, and Minnie Mae moved into the vacant bedroom.

As Elvis settled into his new home he made other refurbishments. He bought a 15-foot long sofa for the living room, with an accompanying 10-foot long coffee table. After reading that President Lyndon Johnson liked to have three TVs on at the same time, Elvis had three sets installed in his own TV room. It also featured a bar and a jukebox — capable of holding one hundred 45s — that was wired to play throughout the entire house. The office building at the back of the building became his business office, managed by his father (Elvis also had his own private office next to his bedroom). The smokehouse was used for storage, and later as a firing range.

Renovations to the property continued to be made over the years. The patio area was eventually covered, first housing an enormous slot car racing track, then remodeled into a Trophy Room, displaying the many awards and honors Elvis had received. A porch at the rear of the house was remodeled and made into a den; an interior waterfall was later installed on one wall of the room. When Elvis became a father, a swing set was promptly set up on the grounds. Graceland was also home to a number of animals over the years, beginning with the chickens that were kept out back

RIGHT: Elvis had Graceland's famous gates specially designed for him.

ABOVE: The TV room, alive with its bright colors, mirrors, and three television

RIGHT: The elegant music room, where Elvis liked to play piano for his friends.

that his mother liked to feed. There were also ducks, turkeys, peacocks, donkeys, a monkey named Jayhue, a chimpanzee named Scatter, and a number of dogs.

One of the nicest additions to Graceland occurred in 1965, when the Meditation Garden was developed. Elvis' interest in the ancient discipline of meditation, and his studies of the spiritual philosophies, inspired him to adapt the existing formal garden at Graceland, "Some place that's really pretty and peaceful where I could think and be by myself." The beautifully designed area features a curved brick wall with stained glass windows fronted by a row of columns, with a fountain that has 14 different sprays and underwater lights, the sound of the running water making the area especially tranquil.

In December 1966, Elvis bought a horse for Priscilla as a Christmas present, and ended up buying horses for all of his friends, which necessitated some changes to the barn and stable area. Elvis could frequently be seen riding his horse around Graceland; occasionally, he rode down to the front gate to talk with the fans who regularly hung out there.

Eventually, he bought a ranch in Mississippi for all his horses. He later sold the ranch, but his favorite horses returned to Graceland — there are still horses on the property today.

The last major renovations to Graceland were made in 1974. Chandeliers were installed in the entrance foyer, over the main stairs, and in the dining room. Stained glass was fitted around the front door, and stained glass windows with giant peacocks were installed in the wall between the living room and the music room. A new color scheme was also introduced to Gracelands. This was the time of Elvis' famous "red era," with carpets and draperies in red, and the furnishings in red and gold; even the grand piano in the music room was gold — although this was later changed for the black Story and Clark baby grand that is there today.

Other rooms were also revamped at this time, each one given a distinct personality. The TV room was given mirrored ceilings and walls, and track lighting. The remaining walls were painted navy blue and yellow, one wall featuring black and yellow

BELOW: The living room, with room enough for everybody on the 15-foot couch.

clouds split by a TCB-styled thunderbolt. The billiard room was given a set of stained glass tiffany lights that hung over the table; the walls and ceilings were covered with 400 yards of multi-colored fabric.

The den also came in for a make over. The thick shag run on the floor and ceiling was now complemented by heavy, wooden Polynesian-style furniture that Elvis had seen in a local shop and bought on impulse. One large chair features Tiki faces along the side; others have dragon heads on the arms. The heavy wooden coffee table and the various animal figurines and statues on the tables and chairs — monkeys, elephants, lions and tigers — led to the room being dubbed the "Jungle Room." The carpeting gave the room good acoustics, enabling recording sessions to be held there in 1976.

The last building added to the Graceland grounds was the Racquetball building. Dr. George Nichopoulos, one of Elvis' doctors, regularly played racquetball and suggested that Elvis take it up as a way of getting exercise. Elvis soon found that he also enjoyed the game, and after playing on local courts, decided to build one of his own in 1975. He added exercise equipment to the building as well, turning it into his personal gym. It was a great place to get in shape prior to a tour, and Elvis played a brief game on the morning before he was scheduled to start a new tour on August 17, 1977.

In October 1977, Elvis and his mother were buried in the Meditation Garden. His father Vernon and grandmother Minnie Mae were later buried there as well. Finally, a plaque was installed in the Garden in memory of Jesse Garon Presley, Elvis' twin brother, who had died at birth. Elvis had always loved showing his home to his friends, and it was eventually decided to open Graceland to the public. Since it was first opened, on June 7, 1982, millions of people from all over the world have visited Elvis' impressive home. On November 7, 1991, Graceland was listed in National Register of Historic Places; on March 27, 2006, it was officially designated a National Historic Landmark.

For the most part, the house was restored to the way it looked prior to the "red era" of the 1970s. The most extensive remodeling took place in the Trophy Room, which was completely renovated, transforming the space into a museum about Elvis and his accomplishments. The trophies are still there: some of Elvis' numerous awards line the walls to

create a "Hall Of Gold." Numerous cases display artifacts from Elvis' life and career. From the family photographs and high school yearbooks common to every home, the displays lead into the early stages of Elvis' career, with his first guitars and records, and memorabilia from all his movies. The iconic outfits on display tell their own stories and exhibits change and evolve. Guests can see many of Elvis' iconic costumes: the army uniforms; the film costumes; the entire wardrobe from the Comeback Special — including the black leather suit; and the tuxedo Elvis wore when he accepted his Ten Outstanding Young Men Of The Nation award in 1971.

The other main renovations were in the Racquetball Building. Not only are the jumpsuits from the 1970s on display, the court where Elvis used to play is now a stunning wall of gold and platinum. In 1992, Elvis' American record sales were updated and recertified by the Recording Industry Association of America (RIAA) for gold (sales of half a million) and platinum (sales of one million) status. On August 12, 1992, a new display featuring 110 awards was unveiled, along with a special nine-foot etched glass award from

ABOVE: Graceland at Christmas – complete with tree and presents.

RCA "To Commemorate The Greatest Recording Artist Of All Time." New gold and platinum awards have since been added, now totaling over 150.

Museums across the street display more of Elvis' belongings; personal items, his cars and motorcycles, and even his planes. But it was Graceland, the mansion, that was Elvis' home, his pride and joy, a special place where he could relax, freed from the demands of his career, and unwind with his family and friends out of the spotlight — having barbeques, pool parties, fireworks battles, golf cart races, horseback riding, or sitting in quiet contemplation in the Meditation Garden.

And now everyone who visits Graceland is made to feel like a friend. As you climb the steps and walk through the front door, you can almost hear Elvis sing, as he sang to so many others: "Welcome to my world."

LEFT: A classic view of Graceland at night, with Elvis' signature pink Cadillac parked out front.

ABOVE: Vernon Presley's vehicle registration for Elvis' pink Cadillac.

ABOVE: Over 400 yards of fabric line the ceiling and walls of the billiard room.

RIGHT: The "Jungle Room," with its Tiki-style décor and animal figurines, conveys a real sense of fun. In 1976, Elvis held recording sessions here.

ALL DRESSED UP

Elvis had a sense of style that was as unique and distinctive as his music, from the raw Hillbilly Cat look of the 1950s, to the groomed, sleek matinee idol of the 1960s, to the jumpsuit-clad super hero of 1970s.

Elvis always took a keen interest in his appearance. One reason he became an ROTC cadet in high school was because of the uniform he got to wear. He never wanted to "dress down"; by high school, his friends recall him wearing dress pants, not jeans. They also remember him constantly combing and adjusting his hair. Elvis let his grow long so he could slick it back like the truck drivers he watched and later became. It was too long for some; in high school, some guys from the football team threatened to cut his hair for him, until his friend Red West chased them off. And he quit another job following too many complaints about his hair length. But Elvis stood firm and refused to cut it.

As Elvis grew older, he spent time on Beale Street, the main avenue for the black community in Memphis, noting what people wore as much as he absorbed the music emanating from the clubs around him. Bernard Lansky, who ran Lansky Brothers' Men's Store on Beale with his brother Guy, recalled seeing Elvis looking longingly through the store's windows at the flashy menswear on display — drape jackets and pegged trousers in bright, bold colors. When Bernard asked Elvis to come inside and take a closer look, Elvis admitted he had no money, but added "When I get rich, I'm gonna buy you out." "Don't buy me out," Bernard famously replied, "just buy from me."

It was the beginning of a fruitful relationship on both sides. His first serious girlfriend, Dixie Locke,

LEFT: Two receipts from Harry Levitch, one of Elvis' favorite jewelers.

RIGHT: Elvis wore this jumpsuit during his Las Vegas engagement in January-February 1970; a picture of him wearing the suit also appears on the cover of his live album *On Stage*.

Elvis Presley

Mr. Elvis Presley
10550 Rocco Place
Los Angeles, California

Diamond Specialists - Fine Jewelry - Unusual Charms

March 20, 1967	to hand make two special horseshoe rings:					
	Ladys white gold horseshoe ring with 10 brilliant dia-					
	monds weighing a total of 1.09 carats					
	Mans white gold horseshoe ring with 10 brilliant dia-					
	monds weighing a total of 2 carats					
	Both rings with Circle G duplicated for authenticity.					
	Made on a net cost plus labor and overhead special.			*E.K. M.L.*	$1659.	00

Purchased by E.P.

Paid 4/6/67 $30 32 ck# 30 04

recalled that Elvis was wearing a Bolero jacket he'd bought at Lansky's on the night they met. Many of Elvis' first stage outfits came from Lansky's, in part because the shop gave Elvis his first charge account: "You got to take chances on people," as Bernard put it. He recalls Elvis having a fondness for the colors pink and black, while trousers from Lansky's, with their inverted pleats and no pockets in the back — "So you could show off your booty when you were onstage," Bernard explained — were perfect for a performer known for his physical exertions in concert. In a few years, Elvis' Lansky threads would go national; for his January 6, 1957 appearance on *The Ed Sullivan Show*, Elvis would wear a gold lamé vest purchased at Lansky's.

Elvis' outfits were designed to attract attention. White shoes and ties would offset dark trousers and shirts. Sport jackets were plaid, checked, or striped. Country singer Bob Luman conveyed just how striking Elvis could look when he recalled what Elvis was wearing at a 1955 gig in Texas: a pink shirt and green coat, red pants, and pink socks. His brown hair was dyed jet black for the film *Loving You*, and he kept it that color afterwards to make it stand out — a look he said was inspired by Tony Curtis (just check out the curly wave in his high school yearbook photo). He took care to dress up his guitar too. By 1955, his guitar had a custom made leather cover, embossed with his name on the front. The cover also had a practical use, helping to keep the back of the guitar from getting scratched during Elvis' vigorous performances.

In 1957, tailor Nudie Cohn designed one of Elvis' most well known outfits, an elaborate gold lamé suit with rhinestone trim. It was a bit over the top even for Elvis, who more often preferred simply to pair the jacket with black trousers. But he created an iconic image when he wore the complete suit, along with gold shoes and tie, in the cover photograph for the

ABOVE: Receipt for rings for Elvis from Harry Levitch Jewelers, Memphis, 1967.

OPPOSITE: The clean lines of this racing jacket, as worn by Elvis in the film *Speedway*, have a timeless, classic look.

LEFT: Elvis frequently accessorized his look with a captain's cap.

RIGHT: In 1970, Elvis began wearing jumpsuits in concert, and they quickly became his signature outfit.

Elvis Presley

Elvis Presley

album *50,000,000 Elvis Fans Can't Be Wrong: Elvis' Gold Records Volume 2.*

Even as a soldier Elvis managed to look sharp. While stationed in Germany he kept several extra pairs of boots and uniforms, so his clothes were always clean and pressed. Post-army, Elvis was no longer a teenager but a young man, and his look matured accordingly. He'd looked profoundly uncomfortable when trussed up in a tuxedo on *The Steve Allen Show* in 1956; in contrast, for his 1960 appearance on Frank Sinatra's special, he slips into his tux with ease.

Sy Devore, who designed clothes for the Dean Martin and Jerry Lewis movies — as well as the rest of the Rat Pack — further refined this more sophisticated look in Elvis' films, describing his approach as "conservative and stylish." Devore's well tailored suits with their touch of Continental flair — seen in such films as *It Happened At The World's Fair* and *Viva Las Vegas* — embodied Elvis' off screen look as well. Elvis never wore blue jeans except in his movies; when he was relaxing, he favored tailored slacks, shirts with collar turned up, turtlenecks, and Eisenhower jackets. He also began wearing hats more frequently, often seen with a black or white captain's cap.

He saw to it that his entourage — friends from Memphis and the army — were dressed up too. Their penchant for wearing similar outfits and matching sunglasses led to the gang being dubbed the "Memphis Mafia" — the most famous group of guys since the Rat Pack. Everyone adopted a Western look when Elvis purchased a ranch in 1967, wearing cowboy hats and boots, leather vests, and even chaps. He became friends with Mike McGregor, a rodeo rider and leather craftsman hired to look after his ranch, who not only designed saddles for the horses, but leather outfits for Elvis as well.

While working on his Comeback Special in 1968, Elvis met costume designer Bill Belew, who would have a big impact on Elvis' look not just during the show, but in his personal wardrobe. Elvis had never looked so good on television. Elvis wears all black in the opening sequence, the tailored shirt and trousers nicely set off by a red scarf around the neck. In the gospel sequence, he wore an Edwardian-styled burgundy suit, again with a scarf around his neck, with Bill opting for scarves over ties to create a more relaxed, informal look. For the final number, 'If I

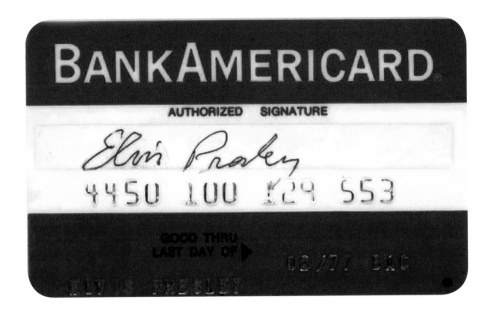

Can Dream,' Bill designed a white Edwardian suit to contrast with the black outfit worn in the show's opening. But his most notable creation was the black leather outfit Elvis wore during the concert sequences, as much of an iconic outfit as the gold lamé suit from the 1950s had been. The suit had a high Napoleonic collar, a look the designer liked for the way it framed the singer's face. It was a look Elvis also liked, and one that would become a prominent feature of his personal wardrobe.

In the 1970s, Elvis added customized accessories to his look. His trademark tinted sunglasses were custom made and featured the initials "EP." He'd always liked jewelry, and increasingly designed items that had a personal meaning for him. He made rings that had his name, or simply his initials. He also designed his own personal logo, placing the letters TCB on top of a lightning bolt, meaning "Taking Care Of Business — in a flash." The logo first appeared on specially made necklaces, which he gave to close friends as gifts; matching "TLC" necklaces (for "Tender Loving Care") were made for women. In 1975, Elvis had a gold ring designed with the TCB logo made out of diamonds; the ring cost almost $40,000.

Elvis' 1970s look is epitomized by the jumpsuit, many of which were designed by Bill Belew; "Elvis had a great body to design for," he recalled. The first jumpsuits Elvis began wearing during his second Las Vegas season in 1970 were relatively simple, with embroidery around the neckline and on the side of the suit. But they became increasingly elaborate over the decade. Jewels soon replaced studs, along

ABOVE: Elvis' visa card, 1976.

OPPOSITE: On stage in a sumptuous jumpsuit in the mid-1970s.

I C Costume Company

6121 Santa Monica Boulevard

Hollywood, California 90038

———

Hollywood 9-2056

Vernon Presley
3764 Elvis Presley Blvd.   Date   August 13, 1973
Memphis, Tennessee 38116

Invoice Number   00372

Job No. 6024

QUANTITY	DESCRIPTION	UNIT PRICE	TOTAL
6	Jumpsuits - re-embroidered, refurbished	$150.00	$ 900.00
1	Jumpsuit - blue & white stripe: removed white nailheads & refurbished		350.00
1	Wht. stretch gab., custom-tailored jumpsuit, heavily embroidered w/stones in Tiger Design w/cape and belt..both heavily embroidered in matching design		2,600.00
1	White stretch gab., custom-tailored jumpsuit, heavily embroidered w/stones in Arabian Design w/cape and belt.. both heavily embroidered in matching design		2,600.00
1	White stretch gab., custom-tailored jumpsuit, heavily embroidered w/stones in Paisley Design w/cape and belt.. both heavily embroidered in matching design		2,550.00
1	White stretch gab., custom-tailored jumpsuit, heavily embroidered w/stones in Indian Design w/cape and belt.. both heavily embroidered in matching design		2,200.00
1	White stretch gab., custom-tailored jumpsuit w/cape and belt..all heavily embroidered w/stones in matching Starburst Design		2,250.00
3	Custom-tailored corduroy suits (2 pants)	750.00	2,250.00

Part show, part pers.

......Continued..

LEFT: Receipt from the Hollywood IC Costume Company for "heavily embroidered" jumpsuits, 1973.

RIGHT: The late 1960s saw a new interest in vintage clothes, as seen in films like *Bonnie and Clyde* as well as Elvis' film *The Trouble With Girls (And How To Get Into It)*.

Elvis Presley

with suits featured embroidered eagles, dragons, or sunbursts on the front and back. Equally bejeweled belts and capes accessorized the outfits. And his boots were designed to match the jumpsuits, featuring studs and often his initials. The scarves were there as well; now they became tokens that Elvis would give to his fans throughout a performance. His hair was big and he sported the sideburns to match. It was a flashy look for a flashy decade, and Elvis was perfectly in tune with the times. And he was always looking for some new way he could dazzle the crowd; he even spoke of designing a jumpsuit that would shoot out laser beams, operated by remote control.

Off stage he was more relaxed, but still dressy. The extravagance of the decade was well suited to Elvis; as his friend Joe Esposito noted, "Elvis did everything in excess." The 1970s was a decade he could have fun with fashion. There were flowered shirts with high collars; scarves instead of neckties; crushed velvet suits; leather coats with fur trim; a suede suit; jackets, vests, and trousers with long fringe. The sunglasses were always present, along with elaborate belts, jewelry, and occasionally a cane. Caught up in the "Blaxploitation" film craze of the period, he adopted a long coat and floppy hat look of the film *Superfly*. He frequently wore a special championship belt that the International Hotel had given him after his first Las Vegas season, featuring a large gold buckle. The clothes of the 1950s emphasized his youth; the clothes of the 1970s emphasized his success.

Elvis he never lost his interest in uniforms: he was thrilled when the Denver Police Force not only gave him a badge from the department, but a full captain's uniform as well, in which he was always proud to be photographed.

Whatever the prevailing fashions, Elvis always wanted to make his own statement. "I guess I always knew if you want to stand out in a crowd, you gotta be a little different," he once said. And Elvis surely was.

LEFT: Elvis in a Sy Devore-designed look for *Viva Las Vegas*.

RIGHT: Elvis in one of his most famous suits, designed by tailor Nudie Cohn.

HAVING FUN WITH ELVIS

If you hung out with Elvis, you never knew what might happen. There might be a fireworks battle on the Graceland grounds. Horseback riding on his private ranch. Or an impromptu visit to Las Vegas on his private plane, the Lisa Marie.

O r maybe it would just be a night out at the movies. Although even that would be a little bit different: most people can't rent out an entire movie house for themselves and their friends, with the snack bar open to all, at no charge. But that's what Elvis, a keen movie fan, did on a regular basis once his fame was such that couldn't easily go to the movies during regular showings. From the mid-1950s he regularly rented out the Memphian Theater in Memphis for private screenings, watching a wide range of films. He especially liked action movies (*The Great Escape, Cleopatra Jones*, the James Bond movies *Dr. No* and *Thunderball*) and comedies (*The Nutty Professor, Cat Ballou, It's A Mad, Mad, Mad, Mad World*). He was a big fan of Peter Sellers, watching *After The Fox, A Shot In The Dark*, and his special favorite, *Dr. Strangelove: Or, How I Learned To Stop Worrying And Love The Bomb*, which he screened several times. Other films he's known to have seen at these screenings include: the horror classic *Village Of The Damned*; dramas like *A Patch Of Blue, Who's Afraid Of Virginia Woolf?* and *Midnight Cowboy*; the modern western *Butch Cassidy And The Sundance Kid*. He also screened *West Side Story* a number of times, repeatedly watching the number 'Cool,' danced by the Jets gang and their girlfriends.

Elvis would rent out other amusement centers in Memphis for himself and his friends to enjoy. He'd frequently patronized the Rainbow Roller Skating Rink before he was famous; now he rented it out and hosted large skating parties. Sometimes the skating got rough; the men would break into two teams and face off, then race toward each other with the intention of knocking down as many of the opposing team as they could. Other times everyone would form a long line by holding hands and skate around the rink at faster and faster speeds, creating a whip-like

effect that would send whoever was at the end of the chain flying.

For outdoor fun, Elvis would rent the Mid-South Fairgrounds, later known as Libertyland. Elvis had always enjoyed the Fairgrounds, going on the rides and playing the games on the midway. Now he would rent the Fairgrounds for the entire night, ensuring that the snack bars were open as well. He especially liked the Dodgem Cars (bumper cars) and the Zippin Pippin, which enjoyed fame of its own as one of the oldest wooden roller coasters in America; this was the ride that Elvis enjoyed the most, riding it over and over again. The Fairgrounds changed its name to Libertyland in 1976; the last time Elvis visited the park was August 8, 1977. The Zippin Pippin was later dismantled and reassembled on the grounds of Bay Beach Amusement Park in Green Bay, Wisconsin.

Elvis also enjoyed watching football and playing touch football with his friends. Eventually, he had uniforms made for the guys that played football with him: blue jerseys with red and white trim, and a bold "E. P. ENTP." (Elvis Presley Enterprises) on the front. In the 1970s, he regularly attended games by the Memphis Southmen football team (later the Memphis Grizzlies).

Even before Elvis made his first record, he told friends that someday he'd be driving Cadillacs, and as soon as the money started coming in he made good on his promise. "The first car I ever bought was the most beautiful car I've ever seen," he said of his first purchase. "It was secondhand, but I parked it outside my hotel the day I got it and stayed up all night just looking at it." Cars were the ultimate symbol of success to Elvis, and throughout his life he continually upgraded to the newest models, in addition to the hundreds he bought for family and friends. But his most famous car is one of the first he owned, a 1955 Cadillac Fleetwood that he painted pink. And a

RIGHT: Elvis with Nick Adams at the Memphis Mid-South Fair on September 29, 1956.

photograph taken by a fan on August 15, 1977, just outside the Graceland gates, shows him in the last car he ever drove, a 1973 Stutz Blackhawk III.

Elvis' interest in wheels wasn't just limited to cars. He was also a big fan of motorcycles; noted photographer Alfred Wertheimer captured a classic shot of Elvis in 1956, looking down at his Harley-Davidson, wondering why it wouldn't start (it was out of gas). Elvis had a preference for Harleys, but while in LA in the 1960s, after riding his friend Jerry Schilling's Triumph Bonneville he decided he liked it so much that he bought one for everyone in his entourage. Elvis and his friends would go for long rides on the Pacific Coast Highway or the canyons of the Santa Monica Mountains, frequently stopping at a market at the top of Topanga Canyon for a soda.

Elvis also owned three-wheeled motorcycles, as well as snowmobiles, refitted to run more easily on the lawn at Graceland. He also liked to zoom around the grounds on a golf cart, and when she was old enough, he bought Lisa Marie a cart of her own. Because he preferred to drive rather than fly to Los

Angeles, Elvis purchased motor homes and buses for the trip, which he then customized, not only with the expected kitchen and sleeping quarters, but also a special hydraulic driver's seat designed to fit his body. The man who customized Elvis' motorhomes also customized a gold Cadillac for Elvis, that featured a record player and television, a bar, telephones, and shoe shine buffer (the vehicle was actually sent out on tour in the mid-1960s, while Elvis was busy making movies). Elvis eventually got over his dislike of flying and bought the biggest thing available on wheels — a jet airliner. He purchased a 1958 Convair 880 in 1975 for a quarter of a million dollars, then spent another $800,000 remodeling and customizing it. When the remodel was finished, the plane, renamed the *Lisa Marie*, had a front lounge, a conference room, and a master bedroom. Elvis referred to the plane as his own personal "Flying Graceland."

In 1967, Elvis developed a great passion for horses. It began when he bought a horse for Priscilla as a Christmas present in 1966. She had so much fun riding it, he decided everyone needed their own horse, and

ABOVE: Holding his ground during a game of touch football – Elvis had special jerseys designed for the guys on his team.

OPPOSITE: Elvis getting ready to take off in his speedboat.

by the end of January 1967 he'd purchased nearly 20 horses. Graceland's substantial grounds had a barn — because Elvis' horse was named Rising Sun, the barn was dubbed the "House of the Rising Sun," a joking reference to the folk song that had been a hit for the Animals in 1964 — but as Elvis kept buying horses, it began to get crowded. In February 1967, Elvis found the solution to his problem, when he located a ranch, Twinkletown Farm, located outside of Walls, Mississippi, and a mere 10 miles from Graceland. The horses were all moved to the ranch, which he renamed Circle G ("G" for Graceland), later Flying Circle G.

Typically, Elvis wanted to share his new interest with his friends, installing mobile homes on the property where everyone could stay, while he and Priscilla lived in the small house that was on the land. For the first half of the year, Elvis spent most of his time at Circle G, buying saddles, tackle and other equipment for the horses, trucks for the guys, and hiring ranch hands to look after the cattle that were also on the property. It was a relaxing period for Elvis, going horseback riding, having picnics, holding skeet-

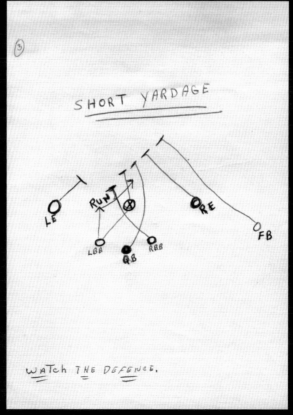

ABOVE: Always interested in outdoor sports, Elvis tries his hand at water-skiing.

LEFT: Elvis' handwritten football plays, mid-1960s.

RIGHT: Registration document for Elvis' horse Rising Sun, 1961.

THE AMERICAN QUARTER HORSE ASSOCIATION

Certificate of Registration

Nick Named - Rising Sun

NAME MIDGET'S VANDY   **NUMBER** P166453

COLOR PALOMINO   **SEX** STALLION   **FOALED** MAY 9   1961

BREEDER LEININGER JAMES V   **ADDRESS** CROWN POINT   IND

OWNER LEININGER LARRY   **ADDRESS** CROWN POINT   IND

SIRE VANDY BEAR   P 73180   **SIRE'S SIRE** LEVAN   P 65698

DAM SALTY MIDGET   P 60288   **DAM'S SIRE** SALTY CHIEF   P   735

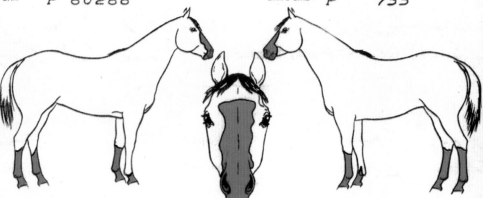

MARKINGS: BLAZE COVERING NOSTRILS AND UPPER LIP
LOWER LIP WHITE   WHITE ON UNDER LIP   SOCK
ON RIGHT FORE FOOT   STOCKINGS ON LEFT
FORE AND HIND LEGS   NO OTHER MARKINGS

This is to Certify THAT THE ABOVE NAMED HORSE IS REGISTERED IN THE PERMANENT REGISTRY OF THE AMERICAN QUARTER HORSE ASSOCIATION.

Howard K. Linger
SECRETARY

DATE: 11 22 61

ISSUED WITH THE RIGHT TO CORRECT AND/OR REVOKE

FRI. SEPT. 25 - 1964

PARIS WHEN IT SIZZLES - PARA - FLAT - 110 min
6 1/2 RI FEATURE — RAN 4 1/2 REELS - 5 1/2 FEATURE

THE ORGANIZERS - CONTINENTAL - FLAT - 126 min
7-R-FEATURE - — RAN ONLY 8 min OF SHOW —

KINGS OF THE SUN - UiA - C-S - — 108 min
7-R-FEATURE - — RAN 48 min OF SHOW —

DR. STRANGELOVE - COL - FLAT - 93 min
5TH TIME —

ELVIS WAS ALWAYS ONE HR. TO THREE HRS. LATE

A SHOT IN THE DARK - U.A. - C-S - — 101 min
SEVENTH DAWN - U.A. - FLAT — 123 min
TOM JONES - LOPERT - FLAT - 131 min
ZULU - EMBASSY - C-S - — 138 min
HELLFIRE CLUB - EMBASSY - C-S - RAN 2 REELS — 93 min
MGM BIG PARADE OF COMEDY - MGM - FLAT — 88 min - BOOKED AT 104 min
FATE IS THE HUNTER - FOX - C-S - — 106 min
GOOD NEIGHBOR SAM - COL - FLAT - 130 min
WILD AND WONDERFUL - UNIV. FLAT - 88 min
CAPTAIN NEWMAN - M.D. UNIV FLAT - 126 min
ALL FALL DOWN - MGM - FLAT - 109 min - BOOKED AT 111 min
WHAT A WAY TO GO - FOX - C-S - 111 min
THE GREAT ESCAPE - U.A. - C-S - 170 min
ALL THE WAY HOME - PARA - FLAT - 95 min - BOOKED AT 97 min
JOHNNY COOL - U.A. - FLAT - 101 min
MARNIE - UNIV - FLAT - 126 min
WALLS OF HELL - HEMISPHERE FLAT - (HOWCO) - 88 min
UNEARTHLY STRANGER - AMERICAN INT. FLAT - 78 min - BOOKED AT 68 min
DR. STRANGELOVE - COL - FLAT - 93 min - 2ND TIME
A SHOT IN THE DARK - U.A. C-S - 101 min
MADMEN OF MANDORAS - CROWN INT. FLAT - RAN 1 1/2 R. - 74 min
ANATOMY SYNDICATE - HOWCO - C-S - RAN 3 REELS - X
DR. STRANGELOVE - COL - FLAT - 93 min - 3RD TIME
KING OF KINGS - MGM - C-S - 5-6-7-10TH REELS MISSING - 115 min - BOOKED AT 161 min
GUNS AT BATASI - FOX - C-S - 1ST RUN - 103 min
SHOCK TREATMENT - FOX - C-S - 92 min
A HOUSE IS NOT A HOME - EMBASSY - FLAT - 97 min - 1ST RUN
RIO CONCHOS - FOX - C-S - 101 min
EMPTY CANVAS - EMBASSY - FLAT - RAN 2 REELS - BOOKED AT 104 min
DR. STRANGELOVE - COL. FLAT - RAN LAST REEL - 4TH TIME
OVER AGAIN - 93 min
BEAUTY AND THE BEAST - U.A. FLAT - 74 min - BOOKED AT 77 min
THE ROBE - FOX - C-S - 133 min
AMERICA, AMERICA - WB - FLAT - 168 min - BOOKED AT 174 min
THE GREAT CHASE - CONTINENTAL FLAT - 77 min
YOUNG SAVAGES - U.A. FLAT - 103 min
SPY HOUSE - M.G.M. C-S - 95 min

---

shooting contests. "There was fun, laughter, and a lot of camaraderie," said Priscilla.

Karate was another big interest for Elvis. He had discovered the sport while in the army, and began taking lessons twice a week in November 1959. He was so taken with the martial arts he continued to train even while on furlough; a photograph from 1960 shows a very serious looking Elvis during a training session with a Japanese instructor Elvis met with while vacationing in Paris. Elvis received his first black belt in 1960, while on May 12 that same year he met Ed Parker, a Hawaiian-born, Los Angeles-based martial artist and instructor. The two men became friends, and Elvis later trained with Parker. He also trained with an instructor in Memphis, Kang Rhee (who gave Elvis the nickname "Tiger"), and frequently attended karate tournaments. Fight scenes in his movies also made use of karate moves. It was an unusual interest — not many non-Asian Americans were familiar with karate at the time.

Naturally, Elvis got his friends and family to take up karate, providing specially designed karate outfits for everyone to wear during training sessions. Priscilla became an enthusiast, training herself and photographing tournaments that Elvis couldn't attend so he could check out new moves by the competitors. He loved to demonstrate his martial arts skills for visiting friends or in the parties held in his Las Vegas suite after shows. The outfit for his 1969 Las Vegas shows had been patterned after a karate *gi*, and karate moves became a regular part of his stage act, causing his drummer, Ronnie Tutt, to take up the sport. "I found that I had to," Ronnie explained. "As he developed more martial arts moves in his songs, I found in order for me to quickly follow him and accent and underscore what he was doing, I became very involved in studying it."

In 1974 he began to discuss the idea of financing, and possibly starring in, a film about the sport. Interest in karate had exploded during the 1970s, due to the success of the films by martial arts star Bruce Lee, and the TV series *Kung Fu*; singer Carl Douglas even had a hit during 1974 with the single 'Kung Fu Fighting.' Ideas were discussed for a documentary, or a feature film, which would have been a good fit for Elvis, due to his interest in action movies. But the idea never got off the ground; fans would have to content themselves with seeing Elvis' karate workouts on stage.

Elvis also took up racquetball in the 1970s, at the suggestion of his doctor. He ended up building a court on the Graceland grounds, complete with weight equipment, a Jacuzzi, and a pinball machine. He last visited the building on the morning of August 16, 1977, hitting a few balls with his cousin Billy Smith.

There was one common element to all of Elvis' off stage interests and hobbies; he enjoyed them the most when he was sharing them with his friends.

ABOVE: Ticket stubs from the Memphis Theater, along with a list of the the movies that Elvis arranged private screenings for.

OPPOSITE: Elvis in his own Messerschmitt bubble car.

Elvis Presley

LEFT: Even while making movies, Elvis could always find time to throw a few balls.

OPPOSITE: Elvis had a longtime interest in karate, having first studied it while in the army.

LEFT: On the go on a go-cart in Graceland's driveway.

BELOW: Another neighborhood game.

RIGHT: A classic look, from the leather jacket to the argyle socks, on a vintage machine.

ELVIS AND HAWAII

Elvis first travelled to Hawaii in 1957; his final trip was in 1977. During that 20-year period, Elvis regularly visited the islands, both for work and for pleasure.

At the time of his first trip, Hawaii was not yet a US state. Elvis traveled to Honolulu by ship at the end of a brief West Coast tour, leaving the mainland on November 5 and arriving on November 9. He stayed at the Hawaiian Village Hotel (later the Hilton Hawaiian Village), which would become his usual base on the islands. Elvis played three shows during his stay; two at the Honolulu Stadium on November 10, and one for military personnel at Schofield Barracks on November 11. The concerts were the last shows Elvis performed before entering the army.

Elvis was interested in appearing in Hawaii again, sending a telegram to his manager in 1959 that read in part "I am in full agreement with you that if all possible we should make our first personal appearance after I return from the army in Hawaii. Perhaps you can work this in with our first tour after we make our first movie next year." At the end of 1960, Parker found the perfect opportunity after reading an article about how efforts to raise funds for a memorial to the *U.S.S. Arizona*, sunk in Pearl Harbor on December 7, 1941, had stalled. Elvis was set to go to Hawaii for location shooting on his next movie, *Blue Hawaii*. Why not arrange a benefit concert for the *Arizona* fund at the same time?

A concert was duly scheduled at Bloch Arena on March 25, 1961. It was Elvis' third concert since leaving the service; he'd performed two shows in Memphis the previous month. Elvis wore his famous gold lamé jacket during the show, and performed an exciting 15-song set, opening with a steamy

BELOW: *Aloha From Hawaii Via Satellite* was the first of Elvis' live albums to reach #1.

RIGHT: The *Aloha From Hawaii* was the first satellite concert ever broadcast, and drew Elvis' largest-ever audience.

'Heartbreak Hotel,' and closing with a frantic 'Hound Dog.' The concert raised over $62,000 for the memorial, and it would Elvis' last show before a live audience until the taping of his *Elvis* television special in 1968.

Hawaii had achieved full statehood on August 21, 1959, and *Blue Hawaii* made full use of the lush scenery on the islands — naturally enough, given that Elvis plays Chad Gates, an aspiring travel guide, who ferries his clients (in this case, a group of teenage girls and their teacher) from one beautiful location to another. The film opens with a panoramic shot of Waikiki Beach, with Diamond Head, a 750-foot high volcanic crater, in the background — the archetypal Hawaiian image. The scenes where Elvis' beach hut was located were at Hanauma Bay, now a nature preserve. Elvis and his girlfriend in the film, played by Joan Blackman, also enjoy a spectacular view of Honolulu from Puu Ualakaa Park.

Blue Hawaii was a huge success on its release in November 1961, its soundtrack quickly going to #1. Due to its success, a return visit to the islands was quickly set up for subsequent films. The next movie with a Hawaiian setting was *Girls! Girls! Girls!*; work began in March 1962, with location shooting in April. Among other locations, the Ala Wai Yacht Harbor, where Elvis' character moors his boats, is easily recognizable. The film opened in November 1962, the soundtrack reaching #3.

Elvis' final Hawaiian movie, *Paradise, Hawaiian Style*, was filmed in August and September of 1965. Throughout this trip Elvis stayed at the Ilikai Hotel, later seen in the opening sequence of the TV show *Hawaii 5-0*. One of the major film locations was one of Hawaii's most popular tourist destinations, the Polynesian Cultural Center, a theme park with seven villages representing different Pacific island cultures, from Samoa to Tahiti to Hawaii. Elvis is shown riding in a canoe as part of the Center's daily Canoe Pageant, while singing 'Drums of the Islands,' and the final production number was also shot at the Center. Elvis visited the *Arizona* memorial during his stay, laying

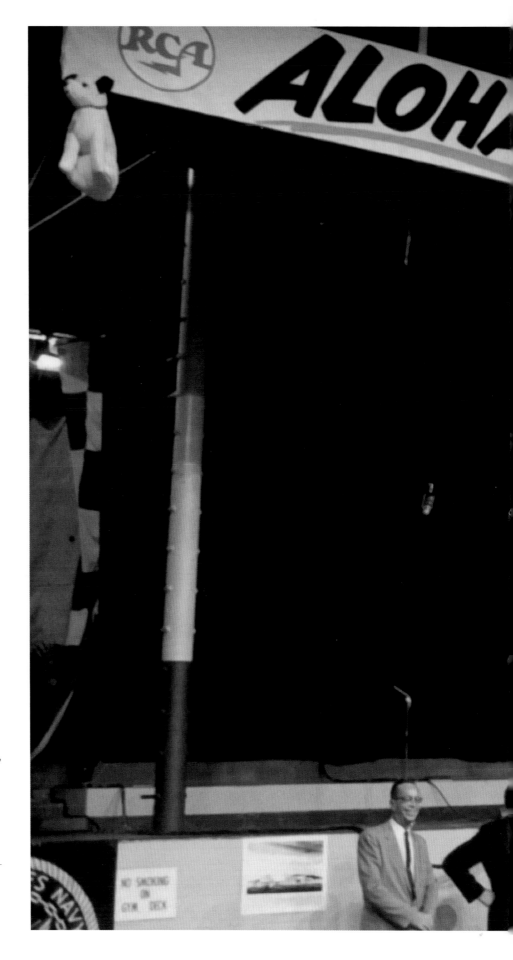

RIGHT: The stage is set for Elvis' benefit concert for the U.S.S. *Arizona* memorial in 1961. The memorial is now one of the most visited sites on the island of Oahu.

LEFT: A panoramic shot of Elvis with Waikiki and part of Diamond Head in the background; a similar pose was used on the cover of the *Blue Hawaii* soundtrack album.

ABOVE: Elvis arrives for his first shows in Hawaii in 1957.

RCA RECORD TOURS
presents
ELVIS
ALOHA from HAWAII
Via Satellite

SUNDAY MORNING
JANUARY 14, 1:00 A.M.
Honolulu International Center Arena

Admission by Donation only
All Ticket Donation Receipts
One Hundred Percent to
KUI LEE Cancer Fund

SEAT 15
ROW 9
SEC. BB
H-1-C ARENA

a wreath of carnations at the site. *Paradise, Hawaiian Style* opened in July 1966, the soundtrack reaching #15 in the charts.

Elvis next visited Hawaii for the purpose of rest and relaxation. In May 1968, prior to taping the *Elvis* special, he took Priscilla to Oahu. During the trip, they attended a karate tournament, hosted by karate legend Ed Parker. There was another trip in May 1969, prior to his first Las Vegas season at the International Hotel, and a subsequent visit that October, paid for by the International, as a thank you for the sold out run.

In 1972, plans were being made for one of the biggest events of Elvis' career. It was first made public on July 8, 1972, when Parker announced that Elvis would perform a show in Hawaii in the fall. It would be broadcast worldwide by satellite as "a way of reaching a larger audience than even his films could," Parker explained. Further details were revealed over the coming months. On September 4, 1972, a press conference was held in Las Vegas where the show's title was announced — *Aloha From Hawaii* — along with a newly scheduled date, January 14, 1973, so as to not conflict with the release of the documentary *Elvis On Tour.* Asked how he felt about performing before a worldwide audience, Elvis replied, "It's

very difficult to comprehend. A live concert to me is exciting because of all the electricity that's generated in the crowd and on stage. It's my favorite part of the business, the live concert."

Though the *Aloha From Hawaii* show had been pushed back, Elvis still performed in Hawaii in the fall, doing three shows at the Honolulu International Center on November 17 and 18. Two days later, on November 20, another *Aloha From Hawaii* press conference was held, when it was announced that the show would be a benefit concert for the Kui Lee Cancer Fund. Kui Lee was an entertainer and songwriter who lived in Hawaii and had died of lymph gland cancer in 1966. Elvis had recorded a beautiful version of Lee's song 'I'll Remember You' that same year; it was first released on the *Spinout* soundtrack. There was no official ticket price; people were asked to donate what they could afford.

After a break for the holidays, Elvis returned to Honolulu on January 9, 1973 to begin preparations for the *Aloha From Hawaii* show, which would again be held at the Honolulu International Center. He had conferred with his costume designer, Bill Belew, about the jumpsuit he would wear; Elvis insisted that he wanted the outfit to have an American theme. Belew came up with what would be one of

ABOVE: Ticket to the *Aloha From Hawaii* via Satellite show, 1973.

RIGHT: Arriving in 1973, with the traditional lei greeting.

Elvis' most instantly recognizable costumes, a white jumpsuit with large bejeweled American eagles on the front and back, matched by an accompanying belt and cape. There was a momentary panic when Elvis gave the belt to the wife of *Hawaii Five-O* star Jack Lord after a rehearsal; an emergency call was made to Belew, who quickly had a new belt made and delivered to Elvis.

A dress rehearsal was held before a live audience on January 12; this show was also recorded as a "back up" performance that could be broadcast in the event of technical failures on the night. The official *Aloha From Hawaii* show began at 1 a.m. on January 14, so as to be seen live on television in Japanese prime time. A festive environment had been created outside the arena, with clowns, bands and other amusements entertaining the crowd. The show would be broadcast live to Pacific Rim countries: Australia, Japan, Hong Kong, the Philippines, South Korea. European countries would see the show on a delayed broadcast that would air later on January 14; US broadcast was scheduled for April 4.

The potential size of the viewing audience, and the presence of the TV cameras, added to the pre-show tension, as the band members recalled. "This is something that's going out all over the world," said Ronnie Tutt, the band's drummer. "You try not to think about it, but it can't help but influence you. Elvis, because of his film experience, would say 'We just wanna go out and do our show, guys. Don't pay any attention to the cameras' — 'those Hollywood cameras,' as he'd call 'em — 'so let's just do what we do, and everything else'll take care of itself.'"

The final show ran longer than the rehearsal show, with a total of 22 songs. Elvis had a new hit to perform, 'Burning Love,' which had reached

ABOVE: Elvis in Hawaii in 1961, when he arrived for the *U.S.S. Arizona* benefit, and to do location shooting for *Blue Hawaii*.

OPPOSITE: Elvis in a dramatic pose during the 1973 *Aloha From Hawaii* concert. His jumpsuit, designed by Bill Belew, featured several American eagles incorporated into the design, as Elvis wanted his costume for the show to have an American theme.

#2 in 1972, and the entire set was geared toward excitement, with uptempo numbers like 'Johnny B. Goode' and dramatic vocal set pieces like 'You Gave Me A Mountain.' A highly emotional 'An American Trilogy' proved to be a showstopper, followed by 'Big Hunk O' Love' and the usual set closer 'Can't Help Falling In Love,' with Elvis so caught up in the moment he threw his cape into the audience (it was caught by *Honolulu Advertiser* sportswriter Bruce Spinks and is now on display at Graceland). It had been hoped the show would raise $25,000 for the Kui Lee Cancer Fund; it ended up bringing in more than $75,000.

And there was still some work left to do. After the auditorium was cleared, Elvis performed five more songs — 'Blue Hawaii,' 'Ku-U-I-Po,' 'No More,' 'Hawaiian Wedding Song,' and 'Early Morning Rain' — that would be cut into the US broadcast. It was estimated that between the three broadcasts (the live broadcast, the European delayed broadcast, and the US broadcast) over one billion people had seen the show. The album, which was released in February 1973, was an immediate chart-topper. It was also released in quadrophonic sound, becoming the first such album to top the charts.

Elvis last visited Hawaii when he flew to Oahu with his friends in March 1977, initially staying at the Hilton, then renting a private house in Kailua, on the west side of Oahu. He paid a visit to the Polynesian Cultural Center, but spent most of his time relaxing on the beach. The laid back atmosphere made Hawaii a perfect place to unwind, and Hawaii's equally laid back residents also allowed Elvis his privacy. "The fans respected him here, and they didn't push," said Tom Moffatt, a DJ who'd met Elvis when he first arrived on the islands back in 1957. "They let him have his space. I think that's why he liked coming to Hawaii."

In 2004, a deluxe version of the *Aloha From Hawaii* shows was released on DVD, featuring not only the original TV broadcast, but also the dress rehearsal and final performances in their entirety. A commemorative statue of Elvis in his *Aloha From Hawaii* jumpsuit now stands outside the Honolulu International Center, since renamed the Neal S. Blaisdell Center. It's not only a tribute to a remarkable concert, but also a testament to Elvis' enduring love of the Hawaiian Islands.

ROCKING THE BOX: ELVIS ON TV

Elvis began 1956 having signed to a major label. The next big boost in his career came when he appeared on television. His 1956 TV appearances in particular made him the most talked-about name in show business.

Elvis' television debut was on January 28, 1956 on the variety program *Stage Show*, hosted by big band stars Tommy and Jimmy Dorsey. Elvis wasted no time in getting down to business, launching into 'Shake, Rattle and Roll'/'Flip, Flop and Fly' with so much energy you can practically see him vibrating. During that song, and 'I Got A Woman,' he steps back from the microphone during the instrumental breaks and begins shaking around in a way no one had ever seen before — a taste of things to come.

Elvis returned for five more appearances on the show, playing a mix of songs from his Sun period, covers, and both sides of his first single: 'Baby Let's Play House' and 'Tutti Frutti' on February 4; 'Blue Suede Shoes' and 'Heartbreak Hotel' on February 11; 'Tutti Frutti' and 'I Was the One' on February 18; 'Blue Suede Shoes' and 'Heartbreak Hotel' on March 17; and 'Money Honey' and 'Heartbreak Hotel' on March 24, all helped push 'Heartbreak Hotel' to the top of the charts.

Elvis was next on *The Milton Berle Show* on April 3, broadcast that week from the deck of the aircraft carrier the *U.S.S. Hancock*. Elvis' (and the band's) growing confidence is evident as they romp through 'Heartbreak Hotel' and 'Blue Suede Shoes,' Bill Black riding his bass like a bull during the latter number. Milton Berle also gets in on the fun, coming out and claiming to be Elvis' twin brother, Melvin, then clowning through a reprise of 'Blue Suede Shoes.'

But it was his next appearance on Berle's program, that created the biggest sensation — and controversy. Elvis sang his latest hit, 'I Want You, I Need You, I Love You.' But what went down in history was his performance of 'Hound Dog,' a song he had yet to record. Elvis was front and center, without his guitar, dancing around the microphone. Then came the song's coda, the tempo slowed down, Elvis bumping his hips and snapping his knees like pistons. It was all meant in good fun; afterwards, Milton came out and again danced around to a brief reprise of 'Hound Dog' with Elvis. But the self-appointed moral guardians of the country saw Elvis' physical performing style as dangerous: "not only suggestive but downright obscene," in the words of one.

This presented a problem NBC, who'd already booked Elvis for another appearance on July 1, this time on *The Steve Allen Show*. There was some thought of cancelling his appearance, but no one wanted to pass up the ratings bonanza that Elvis could bring. In the end, Steve Allen decided to poke fun at the critics by dressing Elvis in white tie and tails. Elvis looked a bit awkward in his formal wear — there's a guitar hanging around his neck during 'I Want You, I Need You, I Love You' that he doesn't even play, and he sings 'Hound Dog' to an actual pooch also dressed in a top hat — but he nonetheless comes through with aplomb. However, he had a message for his fans when he next performed in Memphis on July 4, telling the expectant crowd: "Those people in New York are not gonna change me none! I'm going to show you what the real Elvis is like tonight!"

Finally, Elvis was booked to appear on the country's top variety program, *The Ed Sullivan Show*, on September 9. His segment was broadcast

RIGHT: Rehearsing for his debut appearance on *The Ed Sullivan Show* on September 9, 1956. Elvis' segment was broadcast from Los Angeles, where he was making his first film, *Love Me Tender.*

Elvis Presley

from CBS' studios in Los Angeles, where he was working on *Love Me Tender*, and the show itself was hosted by actor Charles Laughton, as Sullivan was recuperating from an automobile accident. There's no tie and tail this time — Elvis wears an open-necked shirt and plaid jacket. He also performed 'Don't Be Cruel' and debuted 'Love Me Tender' on the program.

He was back on *Ed Sulllivan* on October 28, at what's now The Ed Sullivan Theater in New York (Ed was back as well). He has great fun teasing the audience, laughing during 'Don't Be Cruel,' and the cameras actually show some of his dance moves during 'Hound Dog,' as he skids around the floor. 'Love Me Tender' and 'Love Me' were also performed. Elvis' last performance on the show was on January 6, 1957. He opened with a medley of 'Hound Dog'/'Love Me Tender'/'Heartbreak Hotel,' foreshadowing what he would do with his hits during the concert tours of the 1970s. There are very self-assured performances of 'Don't Be Cruel,' 'Too Much' and 'When My Blue Moon

ABOVE: The more formal look Elvis had during the October 28 show. He performed 'Hound Dog' in a more restrained fashion than on *The Milton Berle Show*.

RIGHT: He is seen here rehearsing for his October 28, 1956 appearance.

Turns To Gold Again' (the camera again safely shooting from the waist up), along with his first performance of a sacred song on television, 'Peace In The Valley.' But the biggest surprise came when Ed came out after Elvis' last song and said: "I wanted to say to Elvis Presley and the country that this is a real decent, fine boy. We want to say we have never had a pleasanter experience on our show with a big name than we had with you; you're thoroughly all right." It helped to put a lid on the controversy about Elvis' performing style for good.

Elvis would not return to the small screen until 1960, when he was the special guest on *The Frank Sinatra Timex Show: Welcome Home Elvis*, shot on March 26, airing on May 12. Elvis made a brief appearance in the opening number, wearing his uniform, but the screaming fans were clearly waiting for him to sing. Forty minutes into the show, they got their wish, as Elvis casually strolled on, now attired in a tux with his hair piled high, cued the band, and sang 'Fame and Fortune.' He begins to loosen up on the second number, 'Stuck On You,' grinning as he provokes shrieks by simply twitching his shoulders. Then comes the terrific encore: Frank returns and offers to sing 'Love Me Tender' if Elvis will take a spin with Frank's hit 'Witchcraft.' It was a great return to the tube, but it would also be his last time on TV for eight years.

Elvis' next television appearances were, however, truly landmark events. In 1968, *Elvis* re-energized his career to such a degree that it quickly referred to as the "Comeback Special." The 1973 *Aloha From Hawaii* broadcast was seen by a worldwide audience. The *Elvis In Concert* special, which first aired on October 3, 1977, captured some of the highlights of Elvis' final tour. He's especially impressive on the more emotive numbers: 'You Gave Me a Mountain,' 'How Great Thou Art,' 'Hurt.' Elvis' TV appearances gave every Elvis fan what they most wanted: the chance to spend the evening with their idol in their very own homes.

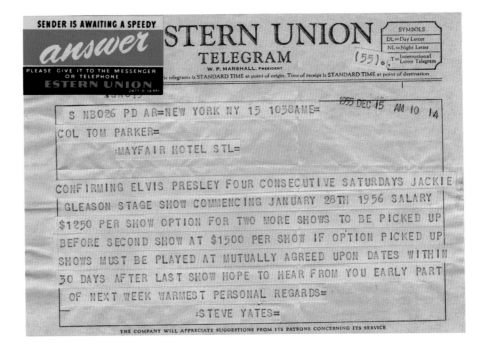

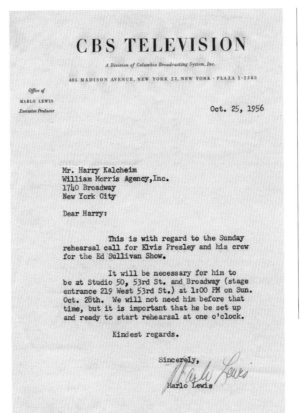

ABOVE: A telegram confirming Elvis' Stage Show appearances in 1956. Elvis made his national TV debut on the program.

LEFT: A letter confirming rehearsal information for Elvis' second *The Ed Sullivan Show* appearance.

OPPOSITE: Another shot from Elvis' October 28, 1956 appearance on *The Ed Sullivan Show*.

LIVE AND IN PERSON

From 1969 onwards, Elvis regularly released live albums, and today you can find live material documenting virtually every stage of his career.

The first live recordings to be released were drawn from the 1968 Comeback Special; a live version of 'Tiger Man,' which appeared on *Singer Presents Elvis Singing Flaming Star And Others* (soon re-released as *Elvis Sings Flaming Star*) and the soundtrack for the special itself. But his first full-length live album was released in November 1969, as part of the two album set *From Memphis To Vegas/From Vegas To Memphis*, later released as two separate albums, *Elvis In Person At The International Hotel* and *Back In Memphis*. The live set drew from Elvis' explosive return to live performance in Las Vegas, and featured 12 songs drawn from four different shows. The excitement is palpable from the very start, with the opening flourishes from the orchestra naturally seguing into a very lively 'Blue Suede Shoes.' Seven of the album's songs are drawn from the 1950s, including three songs Elvis hadn't recorded during that decade, 'Johnny B. Goode' by Chuck Berry, a songwriter whose work Elvis frequently covered, and a decidedly funky 'My Babe,' previously a hit for Willie Dixon. Then there was 'I Can't Stop Loving You,' easy listening country in Don Gibson's original version, later a #1 hit for Ray Charles, and a soulful cry from the heart in Elvis' hands. The album builds to a natural climax, with 'In The Ghetto,' followed by 'Suspicious Minds,' which runs for almost eight minutes, and ending with 'Can't Help Falling In Love,' in place as the standard set closer from then until the end of Elvis' career. The double album set reached #12 in the charts.

On Stage, released in June 1970, was compiled from Elvis' second season in Vegas in February 1970, the tracks coming from four different 1970 shows, and two songs from a 1969 show. Care was taken to not duplicate the songs on Elvis' first live album, and, most interestingly, none of the songs on the album had been previously recorded in the studio by Elvis. The track listing gives a good idea of the kind of songs he was interested in during this period: the heartfelt, dramatic numbers to which he was always drawn ('Release Me,' 'Let It Be Me,' 'The Wonder Of You'), upbeat rockers ('See See Rider'), and numbers that were just plain fun ('Polk Salad Annie'). There was even some insight into Elvis' worldview offered in his version of Joe South's 'Walk A Mile In My Shoes,' a plea for tolerance and understanding which matches the message of 'In The Ghetto.' The album reached #13.

Elvis: That's The Way It Is was also released in 1970, a tie-in with the documentary film of the same name. But it's not quite a soundtrack album; most of the songs are actually studio recordings, with only four songs from the August 1970 Vegas season shown in the film. The live tracks certainly display the power of Elvis' performances before an audience, particularly 'You've Lost That Loving Feeling.' And, as with *On Stage*, the live songs (which also included 'I've Lost You,' 'I Just Can't Help Believin',' and 'Patch It Up') were not ones Elvis had previously recorded in the studio. And some of the studio tracks featured on the album (such as 'Bridge Over Troubled Water' and 'You Don't Have To Say You Love Me') were performed in Elvis' shows. Like *On Stage*, the two records reflect Elvis' contemporary tastes, rather than his 1950s catalogue. The album reached #21.

Remarkably, though Elvis made several TV appearances in New York, he never played a concert in the city until 1972. Which made the four shows he performed at Madison Square Garden on June 9, 10, and 11 a major event, and an obvious choice for a live album. The June 10 evening show was used for the appropriately titled *Elvis As Recorded At Madison Square Garden*, released just eight days after the concert. It was the first live album to feature an entire show, which adds to the listening experience. It was the first time the opening theme for Elvis' shows, 'Also Sprach Zarathustra' (popularized when it appeared in Stanley Kubrick's film *2001: A Space Odyssey*)

ABOVE: *On Stage* featured songs from Elvis' January–February 1970 Las Vegas season.

RIGHT: Elvis in the stunning leather outfit he wore for the 1968 TV special *Elvis*.

appeared on a record, here seguing into 'That's All Right' (soon to be replaced as a concert opener by 'See See Rider'). There were some great new additions to the set, including a steamy 'Never Been To Spain' and a moving rendition of 'The Impossible Dream.' But the new showstopper was 'An American Trilogy,' a medley that combined 'Dixie,' 'All My Trials,' and 'Battle Hymn Of The Republic' in a dramatic set piece that inevitably drew a standing ovation. Balancing the theatrics were bittersweet reflections of 'For The Good Times' and 'Funny How Time Slips Away.' It was an impressive set that handily won over what some had feared would be a jaded Big Apple audience. The album peaked just outside the Top 10 at #11.

Elvis' most successful live album was *Aloha From Hawaii Via Satellite*, which chronicled his *Aloha From Hawaii* show on January 14, 1973; like the Madison Square Garden album, it featured a complete concert.

The album was released before the show was even broadcast in the US, and soared to the top of the charts, eventually selling over five million copies. The set bursts out of the gate with 'See See Rider,' followed by Elvis' latest smash, 'Burning Love,' and his performance of 'Steamroller Blues,' which was released as a single, giving him another Top 20 hit. 'I'll Remember You,' a song by Kui Lui whose cancer fund the show was a benefit, was one of the highlights, as was another song that would come to be as strongly identified with Elvis as it was with Frank Sinatra — 'My Way.'

The final live album to be released during Elvis' lifetime was recorded on March 20, 1974 in his hometown, and titled, naturally enough, *Elvis As Recorded Live On Stage In Memphis*. Elvis is relaxed in front of the loyally supportive home crowd, at one point urging backing singer J.D. Sumner to see just how low a note he can hit. He also has Sumner take

ABOVE and RIGHT: Elvis' 1972 concerts were captured in the film *Elvis On Tour;* albums were also released of two of his shows at Madison Square Garden that year.

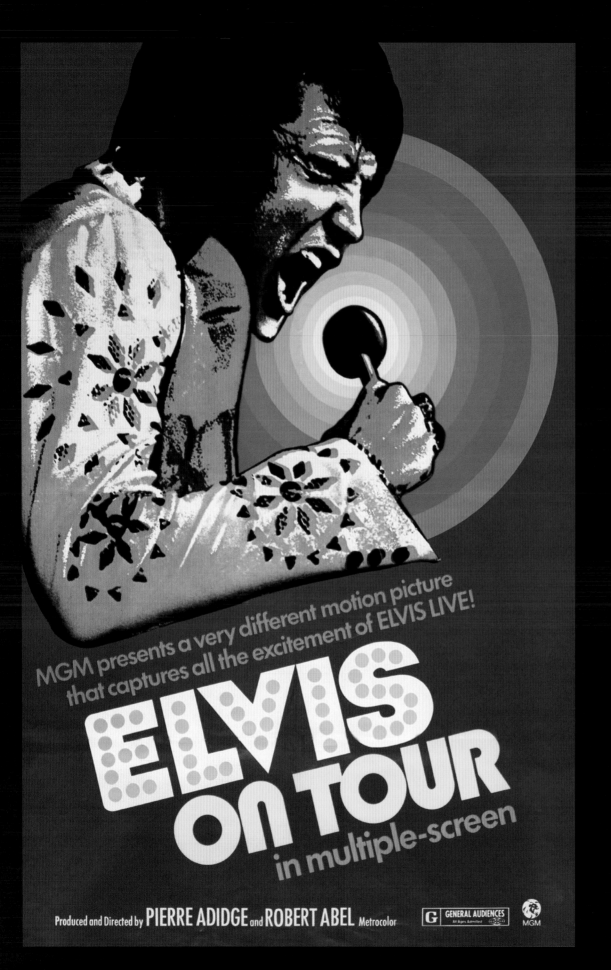

LEFT: Poster for *Elvis on Tour*, 1972.

OPPOSITE LEFT: Elvis as seen during the 'Guitar Man' production number in the *Elvis* special.

OPPOSITE RIGHT: In later years, Elvis no longer wore capes with his jumpsuits.

the opening lead of 'Why Me Lord,' which leads to another song that would continue to be a high point during Elvis' shows, 'How Great Thou Art.' The medleys are especially fun on this release, in particular when 'Blueberry Hill' leads unexpectedly into 'I Can't Stop Loving You.' Released in July 1974, the album reached #33.

Elvis In Concert, released in October 1977, drew on two shows from Elvis' final tour, June 19, 1977 in Omaha, Nebraska, and June 21, 1977 in Rapid City, South Dakota. It's a poignant experience hearing him sing 'My Way' at one of his last concerts, 'Hawaiian Wedding Song' is a nice surprise, and he pulls out all the vocal stops as usual on 'How Great Thou Art' and 'Hurt.' The album is more an overview of a live show than a complete concert, with testimonials from the fans appearing between tracks. Elvis In Concert reached #5 in the charts.

Elvis often said concerts were his favorite part of being an entertainer, and his love of performance shines through on all his live albums.

LENDING A HELPING HAND

Elvis always had a generous nature. As a child, when he had no money to buy presents, he was known to give his own toys to his friends as gifts. And when he began earning a more substantial income, he regularly made charitable donations and performed at charity events.

In 1956, he made a donation to his alma mater, Humes High School, for new uniforms for school's ROTC cadets, and in 1957 he paid for the entire school to attend the annual E.H. Crump Memorial Football Game for the Blind in Memphis, itself a charity event. He was involved in other charity events that year: as the first contributor to Coffee Day for Crippled Children fund-raiser in Memphis, making an appearance at the Shower of Stars benefit for Memphis' St. Jude Hospital (hosted by Danny Thomas and held at Russwood Park), and donating the proceeds from his September 27 show in Tupelo to fund an Elvis Presley Youth Center in his hometown.

Elvis charity shows generated a lot of attention — and donations from fans who were happy to follow Elvis' example of giving. His first big charity show was a July 4, 1956 at Russwood Park in Memphis, a benefit for the Cynthia Milk Fund and the Variety Club's Home for Convalescent Children, before a sellout crowd of 14,000. His first shows when he left the service, in Memphis on February 25, 1961, raised over $50,000 for a number of local charities. His Honolulu concert a month later raised $62,000 to help build a memorial to the sunken *U.S.S. Arizona*. Honolulu was also the location of his most spectacular charity concert, the *Aloha From Hawaii* show that aired on January 14, 1973, that raised over $75,000 for the Kui Lee Cancer Fund. And a May 5, 1975 show in Jackson, Mississippi, benefited the victims of a tornado that had struck McComb, another town in the state. After the concert Elvis proudly presented Governor Bill Waller with a check for $108,860.

But Elvis regularly made donations that didn't received extensive publicity. At the end of each year, he presented different local charities (ranging from 50 to 100) with checks for $1000; in November 1962, Memphis Mayor Henry Loeb presented Elvis with a commemorative plaque

thanking him for his generosity. On June 24 1965, on the film set where he'd just completed work on *Harum Scarum*, a special ceremony was held to thank Elvis for his donation of $50,000 to the Motion Picture Relief Fund, with his *Roustabout* co-star Barbara Stanwyck and Frank Sinatra in attendance. Elvis also made donations privately. When Jackie Wilson — a singer Elvis had greatly admired since he'd first seen him perform in 1956 — had a stroke, Elvis helped pay his medical expenses. Other friends and family relatives benefitted from Elvis in this fashion — not to

BELOW and RIGHT: Elvis in 1956: the same year he became a national star, Elvis also became a regular contributor to charities. The March of Dimes was an organization that was always at the top of the list.

mention the numerous people (some of whom he knew, some he didn't) who received cars from Elvis over the years.

Elvis also understood very well the publicity his name could bring to a charitable cause. In January 1958, he posed for photographs with that year's March of Dimes poster girl, eight-year-old Mary Kosloski. He would continue to support the charity, later having himself photographed when he received his own polio vaccination.

His spirit of generosity lives on in the Elvis Presley Charitable Foundation, which has supported numerous charities, especially those focused on the arts, education, and children's programs. It's a fitting way to honor a man who never forgot what it was like to do without, and never hesitated to take the opportunity to help those in need.

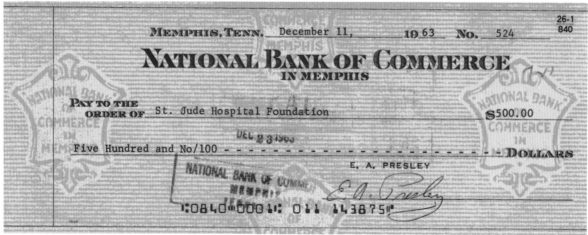

LEFT: Elvis' charity didn't stop while he was in the army; here is a newspaper clipping about his promotion of a blood drive in 1959.

BELOW: A check for the St. Jude's Hospital in Memphis. Actor Danny Thomas helped to raise money for the hospital, and often solicited Elvis' involvement.

OPPOSITE ABOVE: Elvis in the Memphis mayor's office presenting checks to local charities totaling $55,000. Fifty-eight local charities benefited from his donation, December 17, 1963.

OPPOSITE BELOW: Elvis and Danny Thomas; Elvis had purchased President Franklin D. Roosevelt's yacht, the *Potomac*, which he then donated to St. Jude's Hospital.

ELVIS LIVES ON

Elvis was at home at Graceland when he died on August 16, 1977; the cause was later determined to be cardiac arrhythmia (irregular heartbeat). As the news of his death became public, fans from all over the country began to converge on Memphis, holding a vigil outside the Graceland gates, eventually swelling to a crowd of over 50,000. Within a day, every florist shop in Memphis had completely sold out of flowers; 100 vans were needed to carry all the floral tributes to the cemetery. Elvis was interred in Forest Hill Cemetery, in a mausoleum not far from where his beloved mother had been buried. On October 2, 1977, for reasons of security, Elvis and his mother were moved to the Meditation Garden at Graceland.

The following August, fans returned to Graceland for a spontaneous vigil outside the gates, the first step in what would eventually grow to become Elvis Week, an annual celebration of Elvis' life, which today draws thousands of fans from all over the world, becoming so popular there's now also a Birthday Celebration held in Memphis during January. Elvis fans have long been known for their devotion. They love Elvis' music, his films, his sense of style. But Elvis' reach goes far beyond his fan base. His influence began the moment he became a national star, and it continues to this day.

In 1956, Elvis became the world's first rock star, and his success opened the doors for a host of other performers: Little Richard, Gene Vincent, Eddie Cochran, and Buddy Holly, who once said "None of us could have made it without Elvis." Just about every subsequent rock star has acknowledged the influence Elvis had on their careers, from the Beatles to Bob Dylan to the Who to David Bowie. Paul Simon: "Elvis was the reason I picked up the guitar." Janis Joplin: "Elvis is my man." Mick Jagger: "Elvis was and is supreme." Bruce Springsteen put it the most poetically when he told an audience during a show, "It was like he came along and whispered some dream in everybody's ear and somehow we all dreamed it," by way of introducing his next number — 'Follow That Dream,' the title song of one of Elvis' films.

It wasn't just his music that provided inspiration. Elvis' kinetic performing style in the 1950s might have scandalized adults, but it also changed the relationship young male performers had with their bodies forever — a freedom to whom artists like Mick Jagger, among others, owe a huge debt. As James Brown put it, "He taught white America to get down." Conversely, Elvis was also the first to explore a new intimacy in a rock performance. Scotty Moore has described the two performances he did with Elvis for the Comeback Special as the "first *Unplugged*," referring to MTV's program of the early 1990s, that had musicians performing on acoustic instruments. Elvis' performance wasn't entirely unplugged — Scotty was playing an electric guitar that Elvis borrowed during the show — but it did introduce the notion of a major act doing a scaled-down performance, which was a new concept at the time. From the 1970s, arena acts began featuring acoustic segments into their shows, something that's now a staple of rock concerts.

Elvis' image also left its mark, his pompadour, drape jacket and blue suede shoes universal rock 'n' roll symbols: a look that's not just cool — it's classic. The gold lamé suit of the 1950s, the black leather suit of the Comeback Special, and the bejeweled jumpsuits of the 1970s have become equally iconic, and widely emulated. Bono wore an Elvis-style gold suit during U2's *Zooropa* tour. One of the sets for Morrissey's stage shows spelled out his name in large red letters as Elvis' name had been spelled out in the Comeback Special. The British group the Clash were

RIGHT: In October 1977, Elvis was buried on Graceland's grounds, in the Meditation Garden.

THE Hollywood REPORTER

Vol. CCXLVII, No. 44 Hollywood, California, Wednesday, August 17, 1977 Price 35 Cents

Rukeyser granted executive vp status at NBC

M. S. Rukeyser Jr. has been named executive vp, public information, of NBC, it was reported by Herbert S. Schlosser, president and chief executive officer.

Rukeyser will have executive supervision of NBC's departments responsible for press and publicity, corporate and public information, corporate identification, information services and national community relations.

Rukeyser, who has been vp, public information, since September 1974, has been with NBC for almost 20 years. He joined the company in January 1958 as a staff writer in the press department.

Gordon Weaver named Paramount corporate vp

Gordon R. Weaver, vp marketing for the film division of Paramount Pictures, has been named a vp of the parent Paramount Pictures Corp., according to president and chief operating officer Michael D. Eisner.

Weaver now will be responsible for the "overall image of Paramount" through the public relations and advertising departments of all divisions, the company said. He will also continue in his marketing capacity.

Plummer joins MGM's 'Velvet' starting Sept. 1

Christopher Plummer has been signed to join Tatum O'Neal, Anthony Hopkins and Nanette Newman in MGM's "International Velvet." Bryan Forbes will produce and direct this continuation of the studio's classic "National Velvet" from his own screenplay.

Shooting starts in Devon, England, Sept. 1.

Elvis Presley, 1935-1977

By CHARLES A. BARRETT

Elvis Aron Presley, 42, affectionately known as "Elvis the Pelvis," "Swivel Hips" and mostly "The King of Rock 'n Roll," died unexpectedly yesterday at his Memphis home of what was termed cardiac arrythmia (severely irregular heartbeat).

Presley was pronounced dead at
— continued on page 4

HOLLYWOOD TODAY

ABC tops Nielsens .... p. 3
Student wage exemptions . p. 12

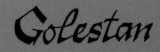

Presley dead

continued from page 1 –

Baptist Hospital in Memphis at mid-afternoon. Police were investigating the possibility that the singer's death may have been drug-related.

A source at RCA Records, the label that Presley had been associated with for the past 22 years, said that the performer was scheduled to launch a new tour today in Portland, Maine. That tour was to have ended Aug. 28 in Memphis.

Presley was born Jan. 8, 1935, in Tupelo, Miss. His first record contract was with Sun Records in 1954. At that time, with a rendition he wrote with an accompaniment from his $2.98 guitar, Presley landed a contract with Sun head Sam Phillips. He first released "That's All Right, Mama" B/W "Blue Moon Over Kentucky," which went on to sell 7,000 copies during its first week of release in Memphis.

RCA bought his Sun contract and released shortly thereafter such successful records as "Mystery Train,"

Under manager Col. Tom Parker, an Elvis Presley concert was unique for at least three reasons – lack of free press tickets, merchandise being openly sold and the shows going off on schedule meticulously.

Parker reportedly insisted that there be no free press tickets for reviewers/critics, even of major daily publications.

Presley's photos and related material were hawked on stage openly and blatantly, with the facility getting a small percentage of all sales.

And during the second half of every concert, Parker would seat himself directly in front of the stage and check on the running time, cueing the show's schedule himself.

"Heartbreak Hotel" and "I Forget To Remember To Forget," as well as "I Was the One."

For a boy who was studying to be an electrician, and driving a truck to support himself, the Sun contract that was bought up by RCA led to a long recording career. As a singer, Presley went on to make a great impact on popular mid-'50s music. His songs like "Hound Dog" and "Don't Be Cruel," among many others, earned him the title of "King of Rock 'n Roll."

His discs were among the fastest-selling in history and one source said yesterday that he sold more records than did Enrico Caruso.

His fame from these records shaped him into a concert, nightclub and TV performer of mammoth proportions. Presley became one of the most sought-after personalities in the entertainment industry. He earned countless RIAA Platinum and Gold records as well as starring in 33 films, including "Love Me Tender," "Lov-

Presley employed no p.r. man, but . . .

Elvis Presley, like a handful of superstars, had no press agent, per se, although RCA Records contributed many stories about his records and personal appearances.

One persistent story over the years had it that a prominent Hollywood publicist continually badgered Col. Tom Parker to handle Elvis's publicity. Finally, Presley's manager said: "OK, how much do you want to pay me?"

ing You" and "Jailhouse Rock," as well as "Viva Las Vegas" and "Charro," which represented a dramatic role for him.

Commenting on the singer's death, RCA Records president Louis Couttolenc said, "Elvis Presley was the greatest legend of the modern entertainment world. The legend is lost to us."

Said Barron Hilton, president of Hilton Hotel Corp.: "We're saddened at the loss of this superstar. Elvis Presley was a great talent and a friend to all of us at the Las Vegas Hilton. There will never be another Elvis Presley."

He is survived by his ex-wife, Priscilla, to whom he was married from 1966 until their divorce in 1975. The couple had one child, a daughter, Lisa Marie, 9.

At press time yesterday funeral arrangements were pending.

FILMOGRAPHY

"Love Me Tender," 20th-Fox (1956); "Loving You," Paramount (1957); "Jailhouse Rock," MGM (1957); "King Creole," Paramount (1958); "G.I Blues," Paramount, (1960); "Flaming Star," 20th-Fox (1960); "Wild in the Country," (20th-Fox (1961); "Blue Hawaii," Paramount (1961); "Follow That Dream," UA (1962); "Kid Galahad," UA (1962); "Girls! Girls! Girls!," Paramount (1962); "It Happened at the World's Fair," MGM (1963); "Fun in Acapulco," Paramount (1963); "Kissin' Cousins," MGM (1964); "Viva Las Vegas," MGM (1964); "Roustabout," Paramount (1964)); "Girl Happy," MGM (1965); "Tickle Me," Allied Artists (1965); "Harum Scarum," MGM (1965); "Frankie and Johnny," UA (1966); "Paradise, Hawaiian Style," Paramount (1966); "Spinout," MGM (1966); "Easy Come, Easy Go," Paramount (1967); "Double Trouble," MGM (1967); "Clambake," United Artists (1967); "Stay Away, Joe," MGM (1968); "Speedway," MGM (1968); "Live a Little, Love a Little," MGM (1968); "Charro!," National General Corp. (1969); "The Trouble With Girls," MGM (1969); "Change of Habit," Universal (1969); "Elvis – That's the Way It Is" (documentary), MGM (1970); "Elvis on Tour" (documentary), MGM (1972).

– continued on page 13

Elvis – country boy unaffected by fame

By MARK TAN

He was a simple, unsophisticated country boy who loved to sing. He grew to manhood and retained that same direct, simplistic philosophy and natural friendliness and warmth, even as the world closed in upon him. Insatiable, the public demanded that every minute of his life be shared – the glorification of the man, the myth, the legend.

Elvis Presley was, in every sense of the word, a true gentleman. He was kind, shy, softspoken, and always generous in both spirit and material wealth, although the latter, to his discomfort, became more publicized and impersonalized than he wished. He was gentle and unassuming; he was as wonderful an audience as he was a wonder of the entertainment world. In Las Vegas, long before Elvis returned to live performing at the then International Hotel, it was not an uncommon sight to find Elvis and his dates and his retinue of friends just "hanging out" at the Aladdin Hotel. Elvis was a loyal friend, and he made hundreds, perhaps thousands, in Las Vegas alone whom he remembered with consideration throughout his career. To see Elvis Presley playing blackjack at one of the Strip hotels and kibitzing with the dealers and customers was seeing Elvis as he was and always wanted to be – just another guy (who happened to be a legend in his own time) seeing the shows and enjoying his brief holidays between movies and recording sessions. It wasn't until after Elvis started making his grueling cross-country tours that he became comparatively inaccessible and invisible.

As in the case of most super-superstars, Elvis, too, lost control of the press coverage he received. To individual members of the press corps, he was forever gracious and cooperative; the unauthorized and often completely fabricated stories, articles, confessions and imaginary "romances" were distressing – when he knew about them – although his staff and friends made every effort to keep him from reading the more hysterical and blatantly false "magazine sellers" features.

When Elvis first started appearing at the International/Hilton Hotel, he almost always "received" the press and friends, VIPs, etc., backstage in his dressing room. He was delighted with his "return" and, occasionally, nervous about future engagements (particularly his first appearance at the mammoth Houston Astrodome that he felt uncertain about filling – and, naturally, without cause). In later appearances, Elvis stayed in his private suite of rooms and "partied" with his pals, invited guests and celebrities. Elvis' famous parties were often attended by dozens of Strip performers, showgirls, dancers, etc., who to this day have (and always will undoubtedly) refused to try to sensationalize or commercialize their friendship with him. Many of the girls he "dated" in Las Vegas who have, over the years, been approached for inside romantic tales have ignored the calls and financially rewarding fees because they valued his sincerity and his almost impossible-to-achieve privacy.

His marriage to Priscilla and her many appearances with him in Las Vegas (he was married in Las Vegas at the Aladdin) were happy and joyous times for both the couple and all the people in Las Vegas who knew them. In later years, Elvis was linked with virtually every available and unavailable female in the world, including Elizabeth Taylor, Bobbie Gentry and Cher. His friendships with other performers are legion, and he delighted in appearing quietly in the back of a showroom to watch one of his pals "do" an Elvis impression. Elvis was – or tried to be – a private man.

Elvis Presley will go on forever and ever. His career, a phenomenon that has never been equaled, will be history as no other entertainer's has ever been or will be again. He was unique, this almost diffident, charming, quietly religious boy who lived in the shadow of his own monumental and staggeringly successful career and legend. He was loved, adored and worshiped in virtually every corner of the globe. He never forgot a kindness, a friend or his fans. And none of us will ever forget him or the brief moments of both personal and professional splendor he brought to the world.

Burrud's ceremony delayed one week

Ceremonies marking the planting of a star on Hollywood Boulevard for producer Bill Burrud, originally scheduled for today, have been delayed until Aug. 24. Burrud's star is located adjacent to Elvis Presley's.

punk rockers, but nonetheless replicated the cover art of the *Elvis Presley* album for *London Calling*. And lead singer Joe Strummer's rockabilly quiff really couldn't have been inspired by anyone else.

Elvis' commercial success also had its impact on the business side of the music industry. Prior to Elvis, no recording artist had ever enjoyed such huge sales. As a result, record companies quickly realized rock 'n' roll was no passing teenage fad, it was a substantial new genre of music. It also opened the eyes of music executives to the fact that commercial success could be achieved by acts found outside the entertainment centers of New York City and Los Angeles. In the wake of Elvis' success, regional scenes began attaining more prominence, something that would benefit musicians based in places like Detroit, San Francisco

and Seattle in the coming years.

And Elvis' Las Vegas shows certainly helped transform the city to a place where rock 'n' rollers are now as welcome as Rat Packers. Until Elvis' return to Vegas in 1969, rock acts didn't feel like they had much of a place in Vegas. "Rockers didn't want to do Vegas because of what they had to do; there was just no real vehicle there of what to do," said Ronnie Tutt, Elvis' main concert drummer from 1969. "And so Elvis established an approach." Since Elvis, it's now become a rite of passage for rock acts to play Vegas, as much a sign of "making it" as playing Madison Square Garden. Which is why when the Cirque du Soleil's lavish production *Viva Elvis* opened in Las Vegas, it felt like a grand homecoming.

But of course, Elvis' most important legacy is

ABOVE: Elvis' memorial plaque in the Meditation Garden, Graceland.

PREVIOUS PAGES: Elvis' death sparked media coverage from outlets around the world.

his music, and acclaim for his work has continued to grow over the years since his death. The 1992 box set *The King of Rock 'n' Roll: The Complete 50s Masters*, a beautifully compiled collection of every song Elvis released during the 1950s, didn't just offer a great way to get all the music Elvis made during his first decade of success in one place; it also provided an exciting illustration of musical history being made — of an artist coming into his own. The Grammy nominated collection achieved record sales for a box set, eventually certified double platinum. The subsequent sets *From Nashville To Memphis: The Essential '60s Masters* (1993) and *Walk A Mile In My Shoes: The Essential '70s Masters* (1995) provided overviews of Elvis' work during those two decades, further helping to put his career into

perspective. And for those who want it all, the 2010 set *The Complete Elvis Presley Masters* contains every recording released by Elvis during his lifetime.

Elvis' music continues to be discovered, and re-discovered. In 2002, a remix of 'A Little Less Conversation' became a chart-topping hit around the world, and was quickly included on the greatest hits collection *ELV1S: 30 #1 Hits* — an album that was itself a #1 hit around the world.

Today, Elvis fans — new and old — continue to arrive at Graceland. During their visits many of them will make a point of writing a comment on the fieldstone wall around his home, moving and heartfelt messages of love and respect. It's a reaffirmation that to millions of people throughout the world, Elvis is somebody who will always be remembered.

ABOVE: Elvis Tribute Artist contests and performances are a part of each Elvis Week at Graceland.

OVERLEAF: Elvis fans raise their candles prior to the Candlelight Vigil held the night of August 15–16 every year at Graceland.

PUT A NICKEL IN (ELVIS') JUKEBOX

Elvis was a collector. So it was natural that when he started to earn some money he began buying records himself, eventually building up an excellent collection.

The 1950s

Many of the records Elvis purchased in 1950s centered around country, rhythm & blues, and religious recordings — the three genres that formed the bedrock of Elvis' musical tastes. But when he played Hank Snow's 'I Don't Hurt Anymore,' 'I'm Gonna Bid My Blues Goodbye,' or 'Just A Faded Pedal From a Beautiful Bouquet' could he have imagined that one day he'd open for Hank — or that he would be managed by Hank's own manager, Colonel Tom Parker? There are numerous songs in his record collection that he would go on to record: Eddy Arnold's 'I Really Don't Want to Know'; Ray Charles' 'I Got A Woman'; Willie Mae "Big Mama" Thornton's 'Hound Dog'; Lowell Fulson's 'Reconsider Baby'; Lloyd Price's 'Lawdy Miss Clawdy'; Arthur Gunter's 'Baby Let's Play House'; Roy Hamilton's 'Hurt.'

Elvis had several of Fats Domino's records, including 'Blueberry Hill'/'Honey Chile,' 'I'm In The Mood'/'I'm Walkin',' 'When My Dreamboat Comes Home'/'So Long,' 'Kansas City'/'Heartbreak Hill' and 'Ain't That A Shame'/'La La,' to name a small number. Fats Domino was in the audience when Elvis returned to live performance in Las Vegas in 1969; at the press conference afterwards, Elvis insisted on getting a picture taken with Fats, telling reporters it was Fats who was the *real* king of rock 'n' roll.

As the decade continued, Elvis kept up with records by his fellow artists on the Sun label: Carl Perkins' 'Matchbox'/'Your True Love,' Jerry Lee Lewis' 'I'll Make It All Up To You'/ 'Break Up,' and 'Lovin' Up A Storm'/'Big Blon' Baby,' and Johnny Cash's 'It's Just About Time'/'I Just Thought You'd Like To Know' and 'Guess Things Happen That Way'/'Come In Stranger.' The new rock 'n' rollers were present and accounted for as well: Gene Vincent's 'Woman Love' and *A Gene Vincent Date*; Eddie Cochran's 'Summertime Blues'; Chuck Berry's 'Carol'; Little Richard's 'Keep A Knockin'.'

Elvis' diverse musical tastes were also evident from the time he began to buy records. He wasn't a big jazz fan, but he nonetheless had a copy of Acker Bilk's 'Summer Set'/'Acker's Away.' He also had the original Broadway cast recording of *The Pajama Game* (whose hit song was the number 'Steam Heat'). A big fan of Mario Lanza, it's no surprise that Elvis owned Lanza's *The Touch of Your Hand* and *A Kiss And Other Love Songs*. He studied the work of other vocalists as well, such as Pat Boone, having 'Cherie, I Love You' and 'A Wonderful Time Up There' in his collection. He also picked up on a vocal trio from Washington state, the Fleetwoods, who had hits with both 'Come Softly To Me' and 'Mr. Blue.' There was even the Chordettes' sweet pop treat 'Lollipop.'

Elvis didn't stop being a record collector when he went into the army. Before he shipped out to Germany, he asked his friend, Memphis DJ George Klein, to send him new releases while he was overseas. George duly sent over singles from the current Top 20 the entire time Elvis was away, keeping him up to date with latest musical trends. His army buddies tipped him to new music as well. Charlie Hodge gave Elvis a copy of *That Golden Chariot* by the Golden Gate Quartet. It was a record Elvis loved, and he would go on to record some of the numbers that appeared on the album, including 'I Will Be Home Again' and 'Swing Down, Sweet Chariot.'

RIGHT: Elvis as the '50s Hillbilly Cat. As he became a bigger star, he continued listening to what his friends on Sun Records were recording.

The 1960s

Rock music went through its greatest changes in the
1960s, creating a lot of exciting new avenues for Elvis
to explore.

The Beatles were the breakthrough story of 1964.
The biggest act in rock since Elvis, he especially
enjoyed their early material, later citing 'I Saw Her
Standing There' as a favorite. His collection of Beatles
records also included 'Slow Down,' originally recorded
by Elvis' Sun Records label mate Carl Perkins. Elvis
also owned *Rubber Soul*, the album that saw the Beatles
moving away from their rock 'n' roll roots, as well as
the single 'Hey Jude,' a song Elvis later recorded and
performed in concert. Another "British Invasion" act
that could be found in his collection was Cilla Black,

ABOVE: Elvis playing his
Gibson J-200, one of his
favorite guitars.

RIGHT: While in the army,
Elvis received records
from the States to
keep up with what was
happening musically.

a friend of the Beatles who was also from Liverpool; Elvis owned her single 'You're My World.'

Elvis always gravitated toward good voices. Dean Martin was one of his favorite vocalists, and he frequently played his album *Dino: Italian Love Songs*. Elvis undoubtedly knew 'You've Lost That Loving Feeling' from the Righteous Brothers' hit version, but he also owned versions by Dionne Warwick and the Blossoms. The Blossoms, who were backing vocalists as well as recording artists in their own right, would back Elvis in his 1968 Comeback Special. Elvis also owned Warwick's album *Anyone Who Had A Heart* and the single 'Always Something There To Remind Me'; Warwick's aunt, Cissy Houston, would back Elvis as a member of the Sweet Inspirations, when Elvis returned to live performance in 1969.

Soul music came into its own during the 1960s, and Elvis was right there along with it. His version of 'White Christmas' was inspired by the arrangement the Drifters had used, and he didn't hesitate on picking up their classic '60s singles 'Under The Boardwalk' and 'On Broadway.' It's also no surprise to find Marvin Gaye's 'What's The Matter With You Baby' in his collection. Or Aretha Franklin's 'I Say A Little Prayer,' Ray Charles' 'Hit The Road, Jack,' 'Crying Time' and *Modern Sounds In Country And Western Music* not to mention Sam & Dave's classic 'Soul Man.'

The folk revival was very much a part of the 1960s music scene, and Elvis was among those followed it. His repeated plays of *Odetta Sings Dylan* led to his own recording Dylan's 'Tomorrow Is A Long Time' in 1966. He also listened to Peter, Paul & Mary, particularly the albums *See What Tomorrow Brings* and *Peter, Paul & Mary In Concert*. And he owned one of the most intriguing songs of the decade; Bobbie Gentry's mysterious 'Ode To Billie Joe.' Instrumentals were also popular in the charts, and Elvis had a number of Herb Alpert's Latin-influenced music: 'The Lonely Bull,' 'A Taste Of Honey,' 'Spanish Flea.'

One of the more unusual records Elvis owned was Charles Boyer's *Where Does Love Go?* He was especially taken with 'Softly As I Leave You,' which he frequently played for his friends, and would later perform in concert, along with 'What Now My Love,' another song from the album. In looking for songs to perform live, Elvis frequently turned to his record collection; both the Bee Gees' 'Words' and Del Shannon's 'Runaway' would be performed during his 1969 Vegas shows. He also had

Jeannie C. Riley's off beat hit 'Harper Valley PTA.' The time he spent in Hawaii undoubtedly influenced him to pick up a copy of Don Ho's 'Tiny Bubbles.' He also had a record by Nancy Sinatra, his co-star in *Speedway*; 'You Only Live Twice,' theme song for the James Bond movie of the same name.

The 1970s

As rock began reinventing itself in the 1970s, artists looked to the past for musical ideas they could work into new shapes — like the British group Mott The Hoople, who were part of the "glam rock" movement, but whose music also had a decided R&B flavor (they even had a song called 'All The

ABOVE and OPPOSITE: Elvis, on leave from the army, at a June 10, 1958 recording session in Nashville – his last before shipping out to Germany.

Merle Haggard's *A Tribute To The Best Damn Fiddle Player In The World (Or, My Salute To Bob Wills)*, and Charlie Rich's *Sings The Songs Of Hank Williams And Others*. 'Dueling Banjos,' from the film *Deliverance*, was a surprise instrumental hit in 1973, and Elvis had a copy of the soundtrack.

The inspiration for some of the country songs that Elvis covered came from his own collection: Billy Lee Riley's 'I Got A Thing About You Baby,' 'Good Time Charlie's Got The Blues' by Danny O'Keefe, and 'I Just Can't Help Believing' by B.J. Thomas (Elvis also had copies of Thomas' 'I'm So Lonesome I Could Cry' and 'Pass the Apple Eve'). Elvis also had a number of other records that would have been interesting for him to cover, such as 'You Don't Mess Around With Jim' by Jim Croce, 'Baby Don't Get Hooked On Me' by Mac Davis, 'If You Could Read My Mind' by Gordon Lightfoot. He was especially familiar with Davis' work since he'd written Elvis' hits 'In The Ghetto' and 'Don't Cry Daddy.' And he did record Lightfoot's '(That's What You Get) For Loving Me' for his 1973 album *Elvis (Fool)*.

J.D. Sumner of the Stamps joined Elvis' live show in the 1970s. Elvis had a copy of the Stamps' 1974 album *What A Happy Time* and the single 'I'll Have A New Song'/'Nothing To Fear'. He also owned many of Sumner's solo releases, including *If We Never Meet Again*, and *The Touch of His Hand, Live...In Nashville*, and *Sing Me A Song About Jesus*. Other religious recordings released during that period that Elvis picked up included Johnny Cash's *The Gospel Road* and *If Nobody Loves You...Create The Demand* by Sammy Hall. Perhaps one of the most unusual records of this type found in Elvis' collection was *The Greatest Love Story: The Crucifixion*, a sermon read by Dr. Jack Van Impe.

He also owned a copy of Les Crane's 'Desiderata.' The spoken word piece, a meditation on finding happiness in a "universe unfolding as it should," was a prose poem written in 1927 by Max Ehrmann, and enjoyed a newfound popularity in the 1970s, with Crane's single hitting the Top 10.

And what were records by the Partridge Family ('It's One of Those Nights') and David Cassidy ('Cherish') doing in Elvis' collection? As you might guess, they were for his daughter, Lisa Marie. And while Elvis wasn't a big fan of disco, he did have a copy of Gloria Gaynor's highly danceable 'Never Can Say Goodbye.'

Way From Memphis'). Elvis had a copy of the band's fifth album, *All The Young Dudes*. Dave Edmunds was a British musician who drew heavily on rock 'n' roll; Elvis had a copy of his first single, 'I Hear You Knocking.' And he also owned of one of Chicago's early singles: the self-described "rock 'n' roll band with horns" released the track 'Free' in 1971.

Country came back in a big way in the 1970s, and Elvis kept up to date with what his favorite performers were doing. He'd already covered Jerry Reed's work in the previous decade ('Guitar Man,' 'U.S. Male'), so it was no surprise to find that he had a copy of Reed's *Georgia Sunshine*. He also enjoyed the tribute albums his fellow performers released:

INDEX